The Drop-In Series

Support Materials Selection Pack

FRANCES WOODWARD

The Drop-In Series: Support Materials Selection Pack
Copyright © Frances Woodward 2018

Illustrations by Alasdair Bright.

A CIP Catalogue record for this book is available
from the British Library

Published by Forward with Phonics 2018

ISBN 978-0-9935873-5-1

Printed in Great Britain

Contents

The Drop-In Series

The books in the Drop-In Series are based around a Community Drop-In Centre in the town of Padly in Dorset. It is a non-profit making business, run for the community, by Sam and Liz Dobson and a group of volunteers.

Sam is the general manager. He oversees everything but is a little disorganised and relies on Liz's quiet efficiency. For anything to do with the computer, Sam relies on Rima. She used to be PA to the boss at a local IT company, so she is a great asset.

Liz runs the kitchen and is helped by Fran and Gwen, who are retired but enjoy the company at the Drop-In and are really appreciated for their baking!

Bill is in charge of the grounds. There is a garden, with a pond and play area for the children. He is helped by Raf, a young Polish lad. Raf is looking for paid work, but he likes to keep busy and knows that working at the Drop-In is helping to improve his English.

Scott is the handyman. He looks after the general maintenance of the building. He does the decorating and mends things when they break.

The Drop-In provides a meeting place for people who want company during the day. People can go there for a meal or just a coffee and a chat.

It is a great place to make new friends and be fed well at the same time!

Characters in the Drop-In Series

Sam Dobson

Sam runs the Drop-In Centre with his wife, Liz. Sam is 59. He retired early from his job as the manager of a DIY store. He was happy when it was a small store and he knew most of the customers. When it was taken over by one of the big companies, the job became very different. He had to meet targets each week and each month and it became very stressful. He decided to help Liz fulfil her dream of helping people in the community by opening a Drop-In Centre.

Sam is a kind, friendly man and enjoys making people welcome at the Centre. He is much happier chatting to people, than doing all the paperwork necessary to run the Centre. He is rather disorganised and forgetful. He needs to make lists to remember the jobs he needs to do. He relies on Liz to be the organiser. He has the help of Rima, who comes in 3 days a week to keep on top of the accounts.

Liz Dobson

Liz is 53. She was the cook at the local primary school for 25 years. She loved her job. She enjoyed making meals that the children liked to eat and would often treat them with a special pudding or cake. They all loved her. When the school had to close its kitchen and buy the meals in from the local secondary school, Liz decided to leave and open up the Drop-In Centre. She knew there was a need for somewhere for people to go during the day; people who need company, want to make friends and have a purpose to their life. It is a non-profit making business because its prime aim is to serve the community.

Liz loves cooking. She likes to be busy. She is very hard working and has lots of energy. She loves organising things and people, especially her husband!

Bill

Bill is in charge of the grounds and garden. He is 72. He was once a farm hand, working mainly on arable farms in the area. He does not care about his appearance. He is always in old clothes and often covered in mud. That's the way he likes it. He has grey, rather untidy, hair, wears glasses and is unshaven. He works hard but can't do the heavy jobs so easily now. He has Raf, a young Polish lad to help him. He takes pride in his vegetable patch, providing most of the vegetables for Liz to use in the cooking. He would like to make the garden completely organic.

Scott
Scott is 33. He used to work for a local builder but was made redundant 2 years ago. He is looking for paid work but enjoys helping at the Drop-In Centre most days. He is their 'Odd Job Man'. He is very practical and can make things, mend things and do the decorating. He has two children, Jack and Emma. He is a single Dad. His wife met someone else and moved to Bristol. Scott likes fishing when he can find the time to go.

Jack
Jack is Scott's son. He is 8yrs old. He is a happy boy and is always telling jokes. He likes helping his Dad at the Drop-In and chatting to everyone there. He is quite sporty, liking football and rugby.

Emma
Emma is Scott's daughter. She is 4yrs old. She is very girly. She likes having her hair brushed and her nails painted. She likes animals, especially Tufty, the Drop-In rabbit, Rex, the dog and Meg, the cat.

Fran
Fran is 60. She is a retired hairdresser. She had her own shop in the town. She is good at cooking and helps Liz in the kitchen with her twin sister, Gwen. She has a husband who is still working and a daughter. She has two grandchildren; Josh who is 3yrs old and Natalie who is 9 months old. She sometimes has to bring them with her to the Drop-In, if her daughter is busy.

Gwen
Gwen is also 60. She is Fran's twin. She likes pink and wears glasses. That helps everyone tell them apart. She likes baking and everyone likes to eat what she bakes! She used to work as a dinner lady at the same school where Liz was the cook.

Josh
Josh is Fran's grandson. He is 3yrs old. Fran sometimes looks after the children for her daughter, so brings them to the Drop-In with her.

Natalie

Natalie is Fran's granddaughter. She is 9 months old. She comes to the Drop-In when Fran is looking after the children for her daughter.

Flick

Flick is a jolly, overweight West Indian lady. She came over from St Lucia with her first husband but they have now separated. She is 50. She has always got a smile on her face. She sees the funny side of life. She is very creative. She does all sorts of craft which she sells on a market stall in town every Saturday. She has always wanted to be a singer. She used to work in the clubs but she got fed up with working in the evenings. She likes playing the drums. She wants to start a choir at the Drop-In. She knows she needs to lose weight, so goes to the Slimming Club at the Community Centre in town.

Jess

Jess is Flick's friend. She is 45. She used to work at the Meet and Eat Café on the main road going out of town. When it closed down, she started helping Liz with the cleaning at the Drop-In. She is very chatty and talks constantly. She is overweight, so goes to the Slimming Club with Flick. They both go to Bingo once or twice a week.

Rima

Rima is 62. She is from India but came to live in this country when she married her husband 40 years ago. She prefers to wear a sari most of the time but sometimes wears western clothes. She is well educated and very good with computers. She was PA to the Managing Director IT Direct, a computer company in Padly. She comes into the Drop-In twice a week to help Sam with the accounts.

Zania

Zania is 13. She was born in Latvia but came to the UK with her parents when she was 4yrs old. She comes to the Drop-In after school most days in order to do her homework. They do not have a computer at home. She is doing really well at school and is very conscientious. She loves animals and takes Rex for a walk most evenings when she has finished her homework.

Taz (short for Tazeema)

Taz is 16. Her family are from Pakistan but she was born in the UK. She does the cleaning at the Drop-In for an hour each evening, after school. She does not get paid but she has a meal instead.

Raf

Raf is 21. He is slim and very fit. He goes running most days and has run a few marathons. He came over from Poland 2 years ago but has not found a permanent job yet. He works in a local bar in the evenings. He would like a job as a landscape gardener but he may have to go to college to get some qualifications. He works hard on improving his English. He helps Bill in the garden at the Drop-In.

Ken

Ken is 54. He is an ex-soldier. He is well built and strong. He used to be very fit but is a little overweight now. He was injured in the war in Iraq and was pensioned out of the army. His right leg had to be amputated and he now has a prosthetic leg. This causes him a lot of pain and he sometimes needs to use a wheelchair for a while. He helps doing odd jobs at the Drop-In whenever he can.

Dan

Dan is 40. He is a painter and decorator. He works for himself. He enjoys helping out at the Drop-In. If there is decorating to be done, he is often in charge but Scott and some of the others actually do the work, as Dan is busy running his business.

Frank

Frank is West Indian, originally from the Dominican Republic. He was brought to England by his mother when he was 11. He is a flamboyant character. He wears colourful clothes, has dreadlocks and a gold tooth visible when he smiles. He is always smiling and laughing. He is an artist. He has a lot of his paintings for sale at the Drop-In and has some in a gallery in town. He has a soft spot for Flick and hopes they might get together in the future.

Ali

Ali was born in this country but his family emigrated here from Turkey. He is 18. He has just left school and is working in McDonald's while he decides what he wants to do. He pops into the Drop-In to meet up with his friend Chang.

Chang

Chang is Chinese. He came to England to do his A levels. He is 18 and is having a gap year before he goes to Bristol University to do dentistry. He likes playing chess and making paper boats.

Fred

Fred is the Fish Man. He is 35. He has his own business. He gets up early every morning to buy fish in the Bristol Fish Market. He then travels all over Somerset and Dorset selling the fish from the back of his van. He is a happy, friendly man who enjoys calling in at the Drop-In for a cup of tea and a chat at the end of the day.

Rex

Rex is Liz and Sam's dog. He is a medium sized, scruffy mongrel. Sam usually takes him for a walk each morning. Zania often takes him for a walk in the evenings.

Meg

Meg is the black and white cat. She lives at the Drop-In and has a cat flap in the kitchen door so she can come and go as she pleases. She helps at the Drop-In by catching mice who like to live in the shed. She also likes catching the birds in the garden, which they don't encourage.

Tufty

Tufty is the rabbit that lives in a hutch in the garden. He is white with a black tuft on his head.

Structure of the Drop-In Series

The Drop-In Series follows the phonic progression as it is presented in the Sounds-Write programme; introducing learners gradually to the English alphabet code.

Level 1 – focuses on the single-letter sounds within 3 sound words (CVC)
6 books

Level 2 – the structure of the words increases to 4 and 5 sound words.
6 books

Level 3 – includes the consonant digraphs.
6 books

Level 4 – introduces the alternative spellings for each of the main vowel sounds. 12 books – 3 books focusing on each of the following sounds: /ae/, /ee/, /oe/, /er/, /e/, /ow/, /oo/ (as in moon), /ie/, /oo/ (as in book), /or/, /air/, /ar/

This book contains support materials for the books that are in The Drop-In Series Selection Pack:

Level 1 – 2 books, Level 2 – 2 books, Level 3 – 2 books, Level 4 – 12 books – one for each of the following sounds; /ae/, /ee/, /oe/, /er/, /e/, /ow/, /oo/ (as in moon), /ie/, /oo/ (as in book), /or/, /air/, /ar/.

The whole series of 54 books plus accompanying support materials can be found on: www.forwardwithphonics.co.uk

If a learner needs to go at a slower pace, needs more practice at each level or needs the progression broken down into more detail, there are more resources in Phonics Resources for Older Learners and Phonics Stories for Older Learners available from: www.forwardwithphonics.co.uk

The Extra Activities section of this book provides ideas for improving the essential skills of blending and segmenting. This type of activity should be used alongside or even before the learner reads the books. The purpose of the books is to consolidate their learning and provide the experience of reading in text.

Ideas for Extra Activities

The activities on the following pages will give the learner the opportunity to practise the skills of blending and segmenting and give them a better understanding of the structure of words.

Word Building

1. Photocopy the sound cards, found at the beginning of each level, onto paper or card, enlarging if required.

2. Laminate if desired. Cut into separate sound cards. Store in an envelope or zip bag, labelled with the name of the book, together with the corresponding word lists for that book.

3. Read the first word on the list and ask the learner to build the word, saying the sounds as they move the cards into place.

4. The learner can then write the word, saying the sounds as they write.

5. When they have completed 5-10 words, ask them to read the words on their list, saying the separate sounds and then the whole word.

Sound Exchange

Sound Exchange is an activity that helps the learner to manipulate sounds in words and to listen carefully to which sound changes when making a new word.

1. Use the same sound cards as for the Word Building activity.

2. Use the word lists found at the beginning of each level. Ask the learner to build the first word on the list, saying the sounds as they build it.

3. Read the next word on the list and ask the learner to swap one sound to create the new word. Encourage them to listen to where the sound changes.

4. Ask the learner to say the sounds and read the word on completion of each new word.

5. Continue through the list. The number of exchanges can vary according to the learner's ability.

Polysyllabic Words

Word Building

The word building activity can also be used to give practice in reading and spelling words with more than one syllable.

1. Make sound cards for each word.

2. Give the learner only the sounds that are needed for the word they are working on.

3. Read the first word on the list, accentuating the syllables slightly, to help the learner identify the separate syllables. Ask the learner to say the first syllable and build it, saying the sounds as they move the cards into place.

4. Repeat the word and ask the learner to identify the second syllable and build it, saying the sounds as they do.

5. When the word is complete, ask the learner to say the sounds and the syllables. When they have said all the syllables, they can say the word.

6. The learner can then write the word, saying the sounds and syllables as they write.

Word Cards

The polysyllabic word cards are included in the Extra Activities section of Levels 2 and 3. They can be printed, laminated and cut up to use as word cards for word reading and writing or for word puzzles, described below.

Word Puzzles

The word cards can also be used as word puzzles:

1. Cut each word card into 2 syllables, to form a puzzle. Make each one a different pattern, as illustrated on the opposite page .

2. These can be added to the envelope or zip bag containing the sound cards and word lists for the Word Building and Sound Exchange activities for each book.

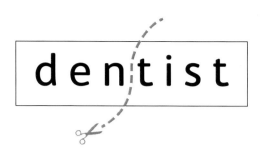 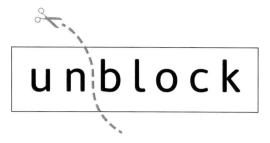

Using the Word Puzzles

1. Ask the learner to find the first syllable of a word by looking for the straight edge on the left and then say the first syllable.

2. They then complete the puzzle by finding the second syllable. They should say each syllable and then the word.

3. When all the words have been completed, the learner can write the words, saying the sounds and the syllables, then the word.

4. As an extra activity for more competent learners, they could then put each word into a sentence.

Level 1

Level 1 focuses on the sound-spelling correspondences and consolidation is achieved by giving plenty of practice and reinforcement. In this level we are predominately using the most transparent aspect of our written code, where each sound is represented by one letter in the context of 3 sound words (CVC). Also included are a few double consonants, which introduce the idea that sometimes sounds are represented by two letters.

Word Building enables the learner to clearly see the structure of the word and gives them practice in the skills of blending and segmenting.

Sound Exchange requires the learner to listen carefully in order to hear where the sound changes from one word to the next. By asking the learner to say the sounds and then read the word, you are also giving them practice in segmenting and blending.

The instructions for two activities can be found on page 11.

The word lists for each activity are on page 16. The sounds needed for both activities can be found on page 17. These can all be photocopied on card or paper, laminated, cut up and placed in an envelope or zip bag, labelled with the title of the book.

Word Lists

Sam and Liz

Words for Word Building:

hat : sun : dog : pan : well : hot : can : big : sit : cat

Sound Exchange Word Lists:

1. sun > bun > bin > big > bag > bat

2. dog > dot >hot > hit > sit > sat

3. wet > well > bell > bill > bit > but

Ken and Dan

Words for Word Building:

dig : wet : bin : mud : pen : cap : red : off : pit : dug

Sound Exchange Word Lists:

1. get > net > not > nut > but > bug

2. man > can > cat > bat > bit > big

3. bun > gun > gut > got > not > pot

Sound Cards

Sam and Liz

w	a	t	s	c	n	d	e
o	g	p	i	u	b	ll	h

Ken and Dan

d	ff	g	w	e	m	b	n
t	u	p	c	a	r	o	i

Sam and Liz

Choose a word for each sentence:

pan	Liz	sun	can	Rex	big

1. Sam sits in the _____.

2. Sam has a _____ hat.

3. _____ is his dog.

4. Liz has a _____ on the hob.

5. Liz gets a _____ to sip.

6. _____ gets the big hat and sits in the sun!

Fill in the missing vowel (a, e, i, o, u) to make a word from the story:

s__n   n__p   s__t   d__g   h__t

p__n   s__p   b__g   h__b   c__t

Copy and read these sentences:

1. Sam has a dog.

_____

2. The pan on the hob is hot.

_____

3. Rex and Meg nap in the sun.

_____

Sam and Liz

h	w	e	g	s	u	n	o	f	m
a	d	v	c	b	y	l	x	h	a
t	i	p	a	n	k	r	p	o	j
y	t	s	e	z	b	u	h	t	n
m	b	i	g	p	s	d	e	g	d
h	i	w	l	s	t	o	y	v	s
p	u	d	m	n	r	g	l	x	i
h	o	b	g	a	i	v	c	k	p
t	w	n	c	p	t	r	a	e	n
o	d	h	m	y	x	a	t	f	j

Find these words:
 sun big
 hot hat
 dog cat
 nap pan
 hob sip

Choose 2 words and write a sentence for each word:

_____

_____

_____

Sam and Liz

Across 3.   2.   4.  7.   9.

Down

1.

2.

5.

6.

8.

Write these sentences:

1. and nap in the

_____

2. has a on the

_____

3. gets a to

_____

Sam and Liz

Put the story in the correct order.
Write the numbers 1–6 in the boxes.

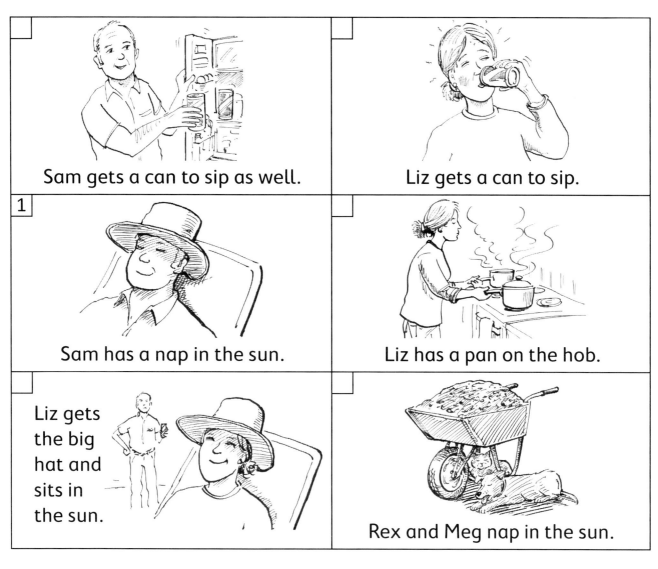

Sam gets a can to sip as well.

Liz gets a can to sip.

1 Sam has a nap in the sun.

Liz has a pan on the hob.

Liz gets the big hat and sits in the sun.

Rex and Meg nap in the sun.

Now write the sentences in the correct order:

1. _____

2. _____

3. _____

4. _____

5. _____

6. _____

Ken and Dan

Choose a word for each sentence:

bag	pen	red	dig	dug	bin

1. Ken and Dan _____ in the mud.
2. Ken tips the can in the _____ .
3. Dan digs up a _____ .
4. Dan tips the pen in his _____ .
5. Ken puts the _____ cap on Rex.
6. Ken and Dan have _____ a big pit!

Find 3 words in the story with <a> in the middle:

_____   _____   _____

Find 3 words in the story with <i> in the middle:

_____   _____   _____

Find 3 words in the story with <e> in the middle:

_____   _____   _____

Choose one word from each line and write a sentence for each:

_____   _____

_____

_____   _____

_____

_____   _____

_____

Ken and Dan

w	d	i	g	f	o	r	l	m	s
a	r	h	u	v	t	e	k	c	p
t	s	z	j	i	n	d	y	a	h
i	x	f	m	u	d	a	l	n	o
n	p	w	g	r	e	c	d	s	t
c	w	e	t	x	k	i	p	e	n
o	b	y	d	w	p	z	n	a	m
r	t	b	j	b	a	g	v	l	c
a	f	i	m	k	n	r	w	h	a
c	h	n	u	p	d	v	u	g	p

Find these words:

dig	mud
can	tin
wet	pen
bin	bag
cap	red

Choose 2 words and write a sentence for each word:

_____

_____

_____

Ken and Dan

Across 3.   4.   6.   8.  9.

Down

1.

2.

4.

5.

7.

Write these sentences:

1. tips the in his

_____

2. puts the red on

_____

3. tips the red in the

_____

Ken and Dan

Put the story in the correct order.
Write the numbers 1–6 in the boxes.

Ken and Dan have dug a big pit!

Ken digs up a tin can.

Rex digs up a red cap.

Ken and Dan dig in the mud.

Dan tips the pen in his bag.

Ken puts the red cap on Rex.

Now write the sentences in the correct order:

1. _____

2. _____

3. _____

4. _____

5. _____

6. _____

Level 2

In **Level 2**, the concept that letters represent sounds is being reinforced but now the structure of the words is more complex. The words contain 4 and 5 sounds with one letter spellings and some two-letter spellings in the form of double consonants.

The instructions for the extra activities can be found on pages 11–13.

The word lists for each book are on page 28. The sounds needed for Word Building and Sound Exchange are on page 29. They can all be photocopied on card or paper, laminated, cut up and placed in an envelope or zip bag, labelled with the title of the book.

Sound Exchange in 4-5 sound words is very limited; when only one sound is being changed each time. Therefore, there are only two changes given in the lists. Follow the instructions on page 11 but this time the learner could write the word when they have built it. When they have the 3 words in a list, they could underline or highlight the sound that has changed in each word. In order to give variation in this activity, because the lists are limited in length, 6 lists of words have been included.

Word Lists

Fran and Gwen

Words for Word Building:

dress : pink : drips : sink : mops : plums : flan : mugs : milk : from

Sound Exchange Word Lists:

1. pink > sink > sank

2. slop > slip > slim

3. milk > silk > sulk

4. from > frog > flog

5. mugs > rugs > runs

6. laps > lips > lops

Rex

Words for Word Building:

jumps : stand : must : spill : smell : just : yells : crisp : drips : rest

Sound Exchange Word Lists:

1. must > rust > just

2. yell > yes > yet

3. prom > prim > trim

4. nest > rest > rust

5. smell > spell > spill

6. jump > dump > damp

Sound Cards

Fran and Gwen

d	ss	p	r	n	e	i	k
l	s	m	f	o	a	u	g

Rex

e	t	r	s	m	i	j	ll
c	o	y	p	u	n	a	d

Polysyllabic Words

The word building activity can also be used to give practice in reading and spelling words with more than one syllable.

The instructions for Polysyllabic Word Building, Word Cards and Puzzles can be found on pages 12–13.

Polysyllabic Words:

Fran and Gwen – apron, mixes, glasses, kitchen

Rex – having, basket, sandwich

Polysyllabic Word Cards

Fran and Gwen

apron	mixes

glasses	kitchen

Rex

having	basket

sandwich

Fran and Gwen

Choose a word for each sentence:

pink	Gwen	flan	twins
help	drips	sink	plums

1. Fran and Gwen are _____.

2. Gwen has a _____ dress and red apron.

3. Fran and Gwen _____ Liz in the kitchen.

4. Fran is at the _____.

5. _____ mixes the eggs and cress.

6. Fran has a box of _____.

7. Gwen puts the plums in a _____.

8. If the milk _____ from the jugs, Meg will lap it up!

Fill in the missing vowel (a, e, i, o, u) to make a word from the story:

tw__ns   dr__ss   p__nk   h__lp   c__ts

fl__n   dr__ps   m__lk   sp__ll   m__st

Practise reading and writing these 2 syllable words:

a-pron   __ _____   _____   _____

mix-es   _____   _____   _____

glass-es   _____   _____   _____

kitch-en   _____   _____   _____

chil-dren   _____   _____   _____

Fran and Gwen

g	b	m	i	l	k	u	j	s	w
a	c	x	p	t	n	r	u	l	f
s	i	n	k	v	e	b	g	m	r
o	t	b	u	y	g	n	s	i	o
f	z	h	k	e	g	w	d	l	m
l	o	p	r	n	s	f	t	w	c
a	k	l	v	e	g	m	o	p	s
n	p	u	t	h	e	l	p	n	y
s	x	m	b	i	k	u	r	d	o
w	h	s	f	m	s	p	i	l	l

Find these words:

help	sink
mops	eggs
jugs	flan
spill	milk
plums	from

Choose 2 words and write a sentence for each word:

_____

_____

_____

Fran and Gwen

Across 2.  3.   4.   7.   9.

Down

1.

5.

6.

7.

8.

Write these sentences:

1. has , has not.

2. cuts the , puts in the

3. If the milk from the , will lap it up.

Fran and Gwen

Put the story in the correct order.
Write the numbers 1—6 in the boxes.

Fran cuts the ham.
Gwen mixes the eggs and cress.

If the milk drips from the jugs,
Meg will lap it up.

Fran and Gwen are twins.

Gwen gets the milk and fills the jugs.

Fran and Gwen help Liz in
the kitchen.

Gwen puts the plums in a flan.

Now write the sentences in the correct order:

1. _____

2. _____

3. _____

4. _____

5. _____

6. _____

Rex

Choose a word for each sentence:

rest	crisps	drips	flan
smell	jumps	spills	tells

1. Ken and Dan come in for a _____.

2. Ken gets a ham sandwich and _____ .

3. Dan gets the ham and egg _____ and a bun.

4. Rex can _____ the ham.

5. Rex _____ up on Dan's lap.

6. The milk _____ on Ken's crisps.

7. Milk _____ from his hands.

8. Liz _____ Rex to get in his basket

Read these sentences. Write 'yes' or 'no':

1. Rex is Liz and Sam's cat.   _____

2. Fran gets Dan a glass of milk.   _____

3. Rex jumps up on Ken's lap.   _____

4. Ken is cross.   _____

5. Liz tells Rex to get in his basket.   _____

Practise reading and writing these 2 syllable words:

hav-ing   _____ _____   _____   _____

bas-ket   _____ _____   _____   _____

sand-wich   _____ _____   _____   _____

Rex

c	r	i	s	p	o	d	r	i	p
v	s	t	k	i	b	s	w	n	l
r	n	h	d	r	i	n	k	u	s
e	i	g	s	a	x	g	r	z	m
t	f	h	j	u	c	n	e	d	e
s	f	u	m	o	s	j	s	f	l
h	a	n	d	i	t	b	t	c	l
x	p	o	r	j	a	m	e	s	h
i	l	f	b	w	n	j	u	m	p
c	r	o	s	s	d	k	c	g	i

Find these words:

cross	rest
jump	drip
hand	smell
crisp	sniff
drink	stand

Choose 2 words and write a sentence for each word:

_____

_____

_____

Rex

Across
2.
3.
4.
7.
8.

Down

1.

2.

3.

5.

6.

Write these sentences:

1. is having a in his

_____

2. gets the ham and egg  and a

_____

3. tells to get in his

_____

Rex

Put the story in the correct order.
Write the numbers 1–6 in the boxes.

Rex jumps up on Dan's lap.

1 Ken and Dan come in for a rest.

The milk spills on Ken's sandwich.

Liz tells Rex to get in his basket.

Liz gets Ken a hot drink.

Ken stands up. His lap is wet.

Now write the sentences in the correct order:

1. _____

2. _____

3. _____

4. _____

5. _____

6. _____

Level 3

In **Level 3**, consonant digraphs have been introduced. This furthers the concept that some sounds are represented by two letters, or digraphs. Each book contains a mixture of the following: <sh>, <ch>, <th>, <ck>, <qu>, <ng>. The spelling <tch> representing the /ch/ sound is also included.

Instructions for Word Building and Sound Exchanges are on pages 11–13.

The Word Lists for each book can be found are on page 42. The sounds needed for Word Building and Sound Exchange can be found on page 43.

As in Level 2, Sound Exchange in 4-5 sound words is very limited; when only one sound is being changed each time. Therefore, there are only two changes given in the lists. Follow the instructions on page 11 but this time the learner could write the word when they have built it. When they have the 3 words in a list, they could underline or highlight the sound that has changed in each word. In order to give variation in this activity, because the lists are limited in length, 6 lists of words have been included

Word Lists

The Trip

Words for Word Building:

rock : clock : stuck : shut : sing : bring : fish : catch : back : song

Word Lists for Sound Exchange:

1. rock > lock > luck

2. stuck > stick > sting

3. shock > sock > song

4. catch > cash > bash

5. sing > ring > rung

Lunch

Words for Word Building:

chat : chin : much : chips : chop : this : then : them : long : bring

Word Lists for Sound Exchange:

1. chat > chap > chop

2. chin > thin > thing

3. bring > bling > sling

4. long > song > sing

5. then > than > that

6. much > such > sung

Sound Cards

The Trip

r	a	s	l	ck	t	u	c
ng	i	n	b	f	sh	o	tch

Lunch

ch	a	l	i	n	m	u	p
s	r	th	e	t	o	ng	b

Polysyllabic Words

The word building activity can also be used to give practice in reading and spelling words with more than one syllable.

The instructions for Polysyllabic Word Building, Word Cards and Puzzles can be found on pages 12–13.

Polysyllabic Words:

The Trip – traffic, rented, children, music, gossip, picnic, unpacks, paddle, catches, bucket, digging, sandwiches

Lunch – Ali, often, menu, chicken, ketchup, having, slimming, salad, sandwich, flapjack

Polysyllabic Word Cards

The Trip

music   picnic

gossip   bucket

traffic   unpacks

children   rented

catches   digging

paddle   sandwiches

Polysyllabic Word Cards

Lunch

Ali

often

menu

salad

having

chicken

ketchup

flapjack

sandwich

slimming

The Trip

Choose a word for each sentence:

songs	clock	chat	unpacks
rocks	bucket	picnic	digging

1. They set off at 9 o' _____ .
2. The children sit at the back and sing _____ .
3. Flick and Jess sit and _____ .
4. "I will bring the _____ box," says Sam.
5. Liz _____ the picnic.
6. Dan and Ken sit on the _____ .
7. Raf catches a crab in a _____ .
8. Rex has fun _____ in the sand.

Add <ck> to these words:

    ro___   clo___   stu___   bla___

Add <ng> to these words:

    si___   so___   bri___   thi___

Practise reading and writing these 2 syllable words:

traff-ic	_____ ____	_____	_____
un-pack	____ _____	_____	_____
goss-ip	_____ ____	_____	_____
pic-nic	____ _____	_____	_____
buck-et	_____ ____	_____	_____

The Trip

v	i	s	t	u	c	k	e	c	d
l	m	u	r	w	h	n	i	l	x
u	b	r	i	n	g	y	e	o	k
n	l	s	t	u	x	b	n	c	e
c	z	i	h	c	t	i	w	k	b
h	k	n	r	a	m	r	o	c	k
u	d	g	e	t	h	n	s	i	l
f	i	s	h	c	f	u	o	w	d
j	v	t	g	h	i	r	n	k	e
k	e	b	a	c	k	j	g	h	b

Find these words:

rock	sing
fish	back
song	clock
catch	bring
stuck	lunch

Choose 3 words and write a sentence for each word:

1. _____

2. _____

3. _____

The Trip

Across   1.    3.    5.   8.   10.

Down

2.

4.

6.

7.

9.

[crossword grid with numbered cells: 1, 2, 3, 4, 5, 6, 7, 8, 9, 10]

Write these sentences:

1. and sit and chat,  has a nap.

2. gets the box from the

3. and sit on the

The Trip

Put the story in the correct order.
Write the numbers 1—6 in the boxes.

Rex has fun digging in the sand.

Dan and Ken sit on the rocks.

1 Sam has rented a bus for the trip.

"I will bring the picnic box," says Sam.

Scott catches a fish in a net.

Flick and Jess sit and chat.

Now write the sentences in the correct order:

1. _____

2. _____

3. _____

4. _____

5. _____

6. _____

Lunch

Choose a word for each sentence:

chin	club	lunch	chunk
crab	chips	brings	chicken

1. Chang and Ali often go to the Drop-In for _____ .
2. Liz _____ them the menu.
3. Chang has chicken and _____ .
4. Flick and Jess go to the slimming _____ .
5. Flick has a _____ salad.
6. Jess has a _____ sandwich.
7. Liz brings Chang a big _____ of flapjack.
8. The jam drips from his _____ .

Add <ck> to these words:

ro___   clo___   stu___   bla___

Add <ng> to these words:

si___   so___   bri___   thi___

Practise reading and writing these 2 syllable words:

of-ten   ____ _____   _____   _____

sal-ad   _____ ____   _____   _____

hav-ing   _____ ____   _____   _____

flap-jack   _____ _____   _____   _____

sand-wich   _____ _____   _____   _____

slimm-ing   _____ ____   _____   _____

Lunch

b	r	i	n	g	f	e	j	x	i
o	g	w	s	a	b	t	h	e	m
c	t	c	h	u	n	k	l	u	z
h	r	o	m	y	d	w	c	m	y
i	t	l	c	t	h	e	y	u	j
p	x	o	v	n	w	i	k	c	p
s	p	n	e	h	s	c	y	h	g
f	u	g	m	c	t	h	s	i	o
i	l	d	w	b	y	a	c	l	h
g	t	h	i	s	f	t	h	e	n

Find these words:

long	this
then	them
they	chips
much	bring
chat	chunk

Choose 3 words and write a sentence for each word:

1. _____

2. _____

3. _____

Lunch

Across   2.   4.   5.   7.   8.

Down

1.

2.

3.

6.

7.

Write these sentences:

1. and go to the Drop-In for

_____

2. has with lots of

_____

3. has a and has a crab

_____

Lunch

Put the story in the correct order.
Write the numbers 1–6 in the boxes.

Jess has a crab sandwich.

[1] Chang and Ali often go to the Drop-In for lunch

Flick and Jess are having lunch too.

Ali just has chips but he adds lots of ketchup.

"This is too much!" say Flick and Jess.

Liz brings Chang a big chunk of flapjack.

Now write the sentences in the correct order:

1. _____

2. _____

3. _____

4. _____

5. _____

6. _____

Level 4 - Ideas for Extra Activities

The concept being reinforced in Level 4 is that, in the English written code, there are many ways to spell most of the sounds. Any activity that highlights the different spellings for each sound will be beneficial to the learner while they read through this part of the series.

Sound Search

1. Ask the learner to list the words in the book that contain the focus sound.

2. The learner can then read each word on their list and underline or highlight the spelling for the focus sound, eg.

   A Day at the Shops:

   d<u>ay</u>

   tr<u>ai</u>n

   gr<u>ea</u>t

   t<u>a</u>k<u>e</u>

   aw<u>ay</u>

3. An alternative way to do this exercise is to record the words on a chart and then isolate the spelling of the focus sound as follows:

Word	Spelling
day	ay
train	ai
great	ea
take	a-e
away	ay

Word Sorting

Another useful exercise to help consolidate the complex phonic knowledge covered in this level is to ask the learner to sort the words according to the spelling of the focus sound, eg.

ay	ea	ai	a-e
day	great	train	take
away	steak	faint	make
stay			late

Word Cards

Word cards of the words containing the focus sound could be made and used for a sorting exercise.

Polysyllabic Word Cards and Puzzles

Word Cards of the polysyllabic words can be made. A line can be drawn between the syllables if the learner needs extra scaffolding to aid the reading of these longer words.

The word cards can also be used as word puzzles:

Cut each word card into 2 syllables, to form a puzzle. Make each one a different pattern, as illustrated below.

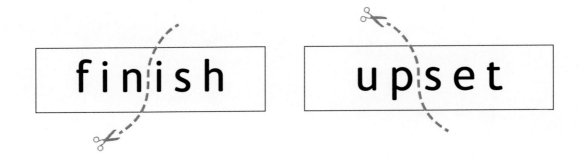

Using the Word Puzzles

1. Ask the learner to find the first syllable of a word by looking for the straight edge on the left and then say the first syllable.

2. They then complete the puzzle by finding the second syllable. They should say each syllable and then the word.

3. When all the words have been completed, the learner can write the words, saying the sounds and the syllables, then the word.

4. As an extra activity for more competent learners, they could then put each word into a sentence.

Level 4 Worksheets

A Day at the Shops

Find the missing word in the story:

1. "We can go on the _____ ," says Liz.

2. "I can take that black _____ back," says Jess.

3. "My _____ is away, so I am a bit fed up!"

4. They met at the Drop-In at _____ o'clock.

5. "Can you take us to the train _____, Sam?"

6. They shop till they _____!

7. "Shall we have _____ in this café?"

8. They have a big _____ of salad but no chips.

9. They have lots of bags of _____.

10. Sam is waiting at the station with his _____.

Find 2 words in the story for each spelling of the sound /ae/:

<ay>	<ai>	<a-e>
_____	_____	_____
_____	_____	_____

Write a sentence for each word:

_____

_____

_____

_____

_____

_____

_____

_____

A Day at the Shops

1.   Who suggests the shopping trip?

     _____

2.   Why is Rima fed up?

     _____

3.   What does Jess want to take back to the shop?

     _____

4.   How many go on the shopping trip?

     _____

5.   What time did they meet at the Drop-In?

     _____

6.   How do they get to the station?

     _____

7.   Why does Gwen want to sit down?

     _____

8.   What does Liz have for lunch?

     _____

9.   Why do Flick and Jess have a salad but no chips?

     _____

10. Does Liz have an expensive watch?

     _____

Practice reading and writing these words from the story:
Write each syllable and say the sounds as you go, then write the
whole word:

hus-band   _____ _____   _____   _____

shopp-ing   _____ _____   _____   _____

chick-en   _____ ____   _____   _____

sta-tion   _____ _____   _____   _____

diff-i-cult   _____ __ _____   _____   _____

ex-pen-sive   ____ ____ _____   _____   _____

A Day at the Shops

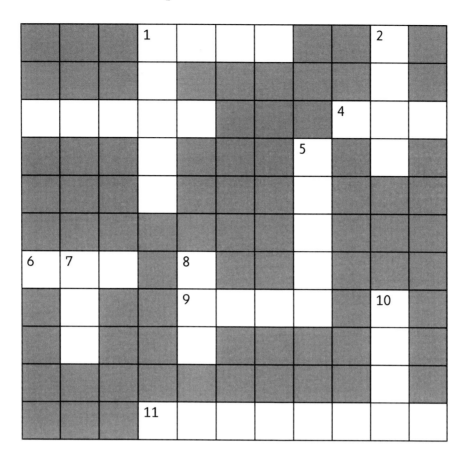

Across
1. A place to have a drink (4)
3. It runs on rails (5)
4. 6 (3)
6. 10 (3)
9. A dull pain (4)
11. Getting thinner (8)

Down
1. Fish and _____ (5)
2. Not fat (4)
5. A flat dish (5)
7. Finish (3)
8. Liz's husband (3)
10. Gwen's twin (4)

Choose 3 words and write a sentence for each:

_____

_____

_____

_____

_____

_____

_____

_____

_____

A Day at the Shops

Number these sentences in the order they appear in the story:

☐ "Shall we have lunch in this café?" asks Gwen.

☐ "Can you take us to the train station, Sam?" says Liz.

☐ They have lots of bags of shopping by the end of the day.

☐ "I can take that black dress back to the shop," says Jess.

☐ Sam is waiting at the station with his van.

1 "Shall we have a day at the shops?" asks Liz.

Now write the sentences in the correct order:

1. _____

2. _____

3. _____

4. _____

5. _____

6. _____

Write about a shopping trip you have been on. Think about:

1. When did I go? Day? Month?
2. Where did I go?
3. Who came with me?
4. What did I buy?
5. How much did I spend?

_____

_____

_____

_____

_____

_____

The Spring Clean

Find the missing word in the story:

1. "I think we will give the Drop-In a _____ clean," says Liz.

2. Fran and Gwen begin in the _____.

3. They _____ the dishes in the sink.

4. They clean the _____ with a damp cloth.

5. "I shall _____ with this big brush," says Fran.

6. "I shall get the _____ and brush," says Gwen.

7. Sam gets the steps to reach the _____.

8. Taz gets a mop and _____.

9. Meg is _____ of the mop.

10. Flick takes the tablecloths off the _____.

Find a word in the story for each spelling for the sound /ee/:

<ee> _____   <y> _____   <e> _____   <ea> _____

Write a sentence for each word:

_____

_____

_____

_____

_____

_____

_____

The Spring Clean

1. Where do Fran and Gwen begin to clean?

   _____

2. Where do they put the dishes?

   _____

3. What do they use to clean the shelves?

   _____

4. What does Fran use to sweep with?

   _____

5. Where does Gwen tip the bits?

   _____

6. How does Sam reach the cobwebs?

   _____

7. Where does Taz clean?

   _____

8. Who is afraid of the mop?

   _____

9. What does Flick do to help?

   _____

10. For how long did Jess clean at the Meet and Eat Cafe?

    _____

Practice reading and writing these words from the story:
Write each syllable and say the sounds as you go, then write the
whole word:

be-gin   _____ _____   _____   _____

emp-ty   _____ ____   _____   _____

happ-y   _____ ____   _____   _____

neat-ly   _____ ____   _____   _____

fif-teen   _____ _____   _____   _____

be-tween   _____ _____   _____   _____

The Spring Clean

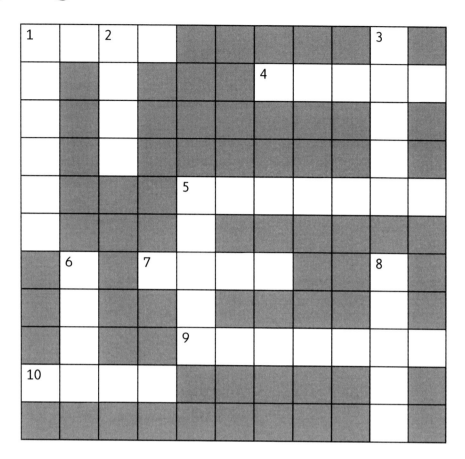

Across

1. A little bit wet (4)
4. You keep things on it (5)
5. 15 (7)
7. You wash dishes in it (4)
9. Liz makes meals here (7)
10. Gwen's twin (4)

Down

1. They stack them in the sink (6)
2. We drink from them (4)
3. We eat off it (5)
5. She goes to Slimming Club (5)
6. 365 days (4)
8. You go up them (5)

Choose 3 words and write a sentence for each:

_____

_____

_____

_____

_____

_____

_____

_____

The Spring Clean

Join the two parts of each sentence with a line:

Fran and Gwen   with a damp cloth.

They stack the dishes   and bucket.

They clean the shelves   off the tables.

Sam gets the steps   begin in the kitchen.

Taz gets a mop   to reach the cobwebs.

Flick takes the table cloths   in the sink.

Write the complete sentences:

_____

_____

_____

_____

_____

_____

_____

_____

_____

Re-write this story adding the capital letters and full stops:

jean is a cleaner she works every weekday but not on saturdays and
sundays on saturdays she meets rashid at the shops on sundays she
has a rest

_____

_____

_____

_____

_____

_____

A Snowy Day

Find the missing word in the story:

1. It is _____ 8th. It is very cold.

2. Sam's _____ gets stuck in the snow.

3. The lock is _____.

4. Fran and Gwen _____ to say they are stuck at home.

5. Scott _____ on the window.

6. "I will clear the _____," says Scott.

7. "I will make you all a mug of hot _____," says Liz.

8. Jack and Emma roll the snow and make a big _____.

9. "_____ your feet on the mat," says Liz.

10. "This is a hot _____, even for me!" says Frank.

Find 2 words in the story for each spelling of the sound /oe/:

<ow>   <o-e>   <o>

_____   _____   _____

_____   _____   _____

Write a sentence for each word:

_____

_____

_____

_____

_____

_____

_____

_____

A Snowy Day

1. How deep is the snow on November 8th?
   _____

2. Why is Sam late getting to the Drop-In?
   _____

3. What does Sam have to do to the lock?
   _____

4. Why are Fran and Gwen stuck at home?
   _____

5. Who taps on the window?
   _____

6. Do Jack and Emma help to clear the snow?
   _____

7. What do they use for the snowman's nose?
   _____

8. What does Liz ask them to do when they come into the kitchen?
   _____

9. What time does Frank come in for his lunch?
   _____

10. What does Liz make for lunch?
    _____

Practice reading and writing these words from the story:
Write each syllable and say the sounds as you go, then write the
whole word:

bus-es   _____ _____   _____   _____

froz-en   _____ _____   _____   _____

traff-ic   _____ _____   _____   _____

snow-man   _____ _____   _____   _____

No-vem-ber   ____ _____ _____   _____   _____

choc-o-late   _____ __ _____   _____   _____

A Snowy Day

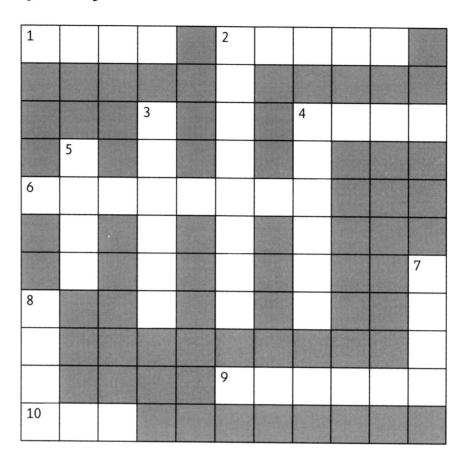

Across
1. A dish (4)
2. Bang your feet (5)
4. Not hot (4)
6. After October (8)
9. Made of glass (6)
10. You lock with it (3)

Down
2. A round lump of snow (8)
3. 12 (6)
4. Orange vegetable (6)
5. Where we live (4)
7. Not fast (4)
8. Make safe (4)

Choose 3 words and write a sentence for each:

_____

_____

_____

_____

_____

_____

_____

_____

_____

A Snowy Day

Number these sentences in the order they appear in the story:

☐ "I will clear the snow," says Scott.

☐ "Don't bring that snow into the kitchen," says Liz.

1 It was November 8th.

☐ "Let's all have a bowl of curry," says Liz.

☐ Sam's van gets stuck in the snow.

☐ Jack and Emma throw snowballs and make a mess.

Now write the sentences in the correct order:

1. _____

2. _____

3. _____

4. _____

5. _____

6. _____

Write about a snowy day. Think about:

1. Do you like the snow?

2. Did you go out in it?

3. Did it stop the traffic?

4. What did you wear?

5. Did you make a snowman?

_____

_____

_____

_____

_____

The Circus

Find the missing word in the story:

1   "It is my birthday on _____," said Flick.

2   There is a _____ in a big tent near the river.

3   Flick put on a _____ and jumper.

4   They got some _____ and searched for their seats.

5   There were jugglers and _____.

6   A girl was on a _____ at the top of the Big Top.

7   Then she held on with her _____.

8   The men had made _____ and chips for everyone.

9   There was a big cake with _____ candles on it.

10 "So – my age is no longer a _____!" said Flick.

Find a word in the story for each spelling for the sound /er/:

<er> _____   <ur> _____   <ir> _____   <ear> _____

Write a sentence for each word:

_____

_____

_____

_____

_____

_____

_____

_____

The Circus

1. On which day was it Flick's birthday?

    _____

2. What was in a big tent near the river?

    _____

3. What had Flick's brother sent for her birthday?

    _____

4. Where did Flick meet the others?

    _____

5. What did they get before going to their seats?

    _____

6. What was the girl doing at the top of the Big Top?

    _____

7. What saved her when she fell?

    _____

8. Did Fran think the girl was brave or stupid?

    _____

9. What had the men made for them when they got back?

    _____

10. How many candles did the cake have on it?

    _____

Practice reading and writing these words from the story:
Write each syllable and say the sounds as you go, then write the
whole word:

cir-cus   _____ _____   _____   _____

fif-ty   _____ _____   _____   _____

trap-eze   _____ _____   _____   _____

Thurs-day   _____ _____   _____   _____

ac-ro-bat   ____ ___ _____   _____   _____

cel-e-brate   _____ __ _____ _____   _____

The Circus

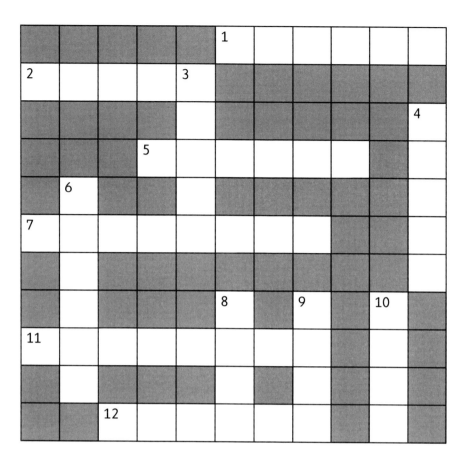

Across
1. Meat in a roll (6)
2. Item of ladies' clothing (5)
5. A fact kept quiet (6)
7. The day of your birth (8)
11. Something not expected (8)
12. They join your leg and foot (6)

Down
3. We use them to bite (5)
4. 50 (5)
6. Seen in a tent (6)
8. Not a boy (4)
9. We stand on them (4)
10. Name of the circus (4)

Choose 3 words and write a sentence for each:

_____

_____

_____

_____

_____

_____

_____

_____

_____

The Circus

Join the two parts of each sentence with a line:

"It's my birthday   and searched for their seats.

There is a circus in   with fifty candles on it.

They got some sweets   burgers and chips.

There were jugglers   a big tent near the river.

The men had made   on Thursday," said Flick.

There was a big cake   and acrobats.

Write the complete sentences:

_____

_____

_____

_____

_____

_____

_____

_____

_____

Re-write this story adding the capital letters and full stops:

it was jen's birthday last sunday she was 28 her husband, max, made her a cake with 28 candles on it in the evening they went to a show in london

_____

_____

_____

_____

_____

_____

_____

The Picnic

Find the missing word in the story:

1. This is the hottest _____ we have had for years.

2. "Let's have a _____ for lunch," says Sam.

3. Gwen makes an egg and _____ flan.

4. Liz spreads soft cheese on some _____.

5. Fran spreads jam on some _____.

6. They have cans of drink in a _____ filled with ice.

7. "We are meant to be on a _____!" says Jess.

8. _____ runs off with a chicken leg.

9. Emma hits Jack for making her _____ soggy.

10. "Perhaps a picnic was not such a good _____," says Sam.

Underline the spelling for the sound /e/ in these words:

head	many	help	weather	bench	said

Write a sentence for each word:

_____

_____

_____

_____

_____

_____

_____

_____

The Picnic

1. What was the weather like in May?

    _____

2. What does Sam suggest doing for lunch?

    _____

3. What does Gwen make for the picnic?

    _____

4. What does Fran spread on the scones?

    _____

5. Where does Liz say lunch will be?

    _____

6. Where are the cans of drink?

    _____

7. Who helped Flick lift the bench?

    _____

8. Why does Raf want a healthy lunch?

    _____

9. Where do the feathers come from?

    _____

10. How does Emma's pizza get soggy?

    _____

Practice reading and writing these words from the story:
Write each syllable and say the sounds as you go, then write the whole word:

pic-nic   _____ _____   _____   _____

win-ter   _____ _____   _____   _____

per-haps   _____ _____   _____   _____

dread-ful   _____ _____   _____   _____

a-maz-ing   __ _____ ___   _____   _____

mar-a-thon   _____ __ _____   _____   _____

The Picnic

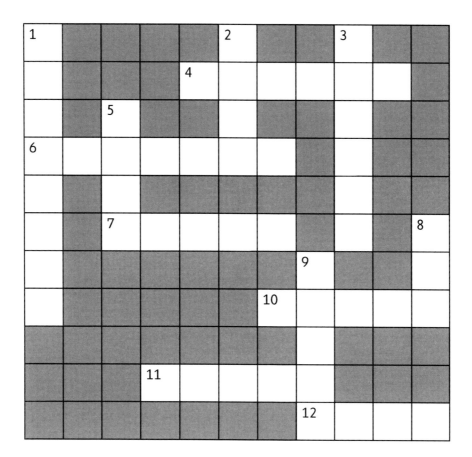

Across

4. A meal outside (6)
6. Needing a drink (7)
7. Put foot down (5)
10. Very wet (5)
11. Made from potatoes (5)
12. Used for carrying things (4)

Down

1. Birds have them (8)
2. Pick up (4)
3. Cold season (6)
5. Eating to slim (4)
8. The 5th month (3)
9. Cooked in the oven (5)

Choose 3 words and write a sentence for each:

_____

_____

_____

_____

_____

_____

_____

_____

The Picnic

Number these sentences in the order they appear in the story:

☐ Jack trips over the bucket of drinks.

☐ Gwen makes an egg and cheese flan.

☐ 1 "Let's have a picnic for lunch," says Sam.

☐ "Help me bring the bench over, Raf," says Flick.

☐ "Let's go in," says Sam.

☐ Meg licks the butter from the buns.

Now write the sentences in the correct order:

1. _____

2. _____

3. _____

4. _____

5. _____

6. _____

Write about a picnic. Think about:

1. When did you have a picnic?

2. Where did you go?

3. What food did you have?

4. What did you have to drink?

5. Did you enjoy it?

_____

_____

_____

_____

The Swim

Find the missing word in the story:

1. "Flick and I are going for a _____," says Jess.

2. "I must peg out these _____ first," says Liz.

3. The ladies meet in _____ at 10.30am.

4. They _____ in and make a big splash!

5. Fran and _____ swim a little and chat a lot!

6. "I have to keep my feet on the _____," says Fran.

7. "How many _____ did we do?" asks Jess.

8. "_____ Club will be pleased with you," says Liz.

9. They get their _____ from the lockers.

10. "Shall we have a _____?" asks Jess.

Find 3 words in the story for each spelling of the sound /ow/:

<ow> _____ _____ _____

<ou> _____ _____ _____

Write a sentence for each word:

_____

_____

_____

_____

_____

_____

_____

_____

_____

The Swim

1. Where are Flick and Jess going?

    _____

2. What does Liz have to do first?

    _____

3. At what time do the ladies meet?

    _____

4. Where do they put their clothes?

    _____

5. Do Flick and Jess swim a lot?

    _____

6. Why does Fran not like to go to the deep end?

    _____

7. How many lengths do Flick and Jess do?

    _____

8. Why is swimming good for you?

    _____

9. What do they do before they get dressed?

    _____

10. Do Flick and Jess have cake with their coffee?

    _____

Practice reading and writing these words from the story:
Write each syllable and say the sounds as you go, then write the whole word:

six-ty   _____ _____ _____ _____

tow-el   _____ _____ _____ _____

coff-ee   _____ _____ _____ _____

cow-ard   _____ _____ _____ _____

de-serve   ____ _____ _____ _____

a-ny-one   ___ ___ _____ _____ _____

The Swim

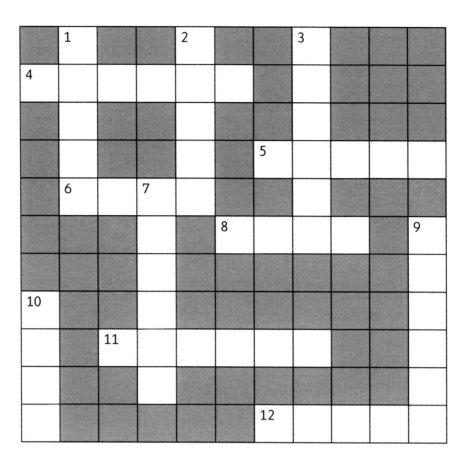

Across
4. Not brave (6)
5. 60 (5)
6. Lots of houses and shops (4)
8. Cannot be found (4)
11. Spray of water overhead (6)
12. We live in it (5)

Down
1. Say numbers one at a time (5)
2. Die in water (5)
3. Not men (6)
7. How heavy you are (6)
9. Drink made from a bean (6)
10. Move in water (4)

Choose 3 words and write a sentence for each:

_____
_____
_____
_____
_____
_____
_____
_____
_____

The Swim

Join the two parts of each sentence with a line:

"Flick and I are going   in case I drown."

They get changed and   for a swim."

Fran and Gwen swim a little   a swim."

"I do not go to the deep end   and chat a lot!

They get their towels   put their clothes in the lockers.

"I feel so much better after   from the lockers.

Write the complete sentences:

_____

_____

_____

_____

_____

_____

_____

_____

_____

Re-write this story adding the capital letters and full stops:

every wednesday I go swimming I meet sally and ann there we swim
lots of lengths on saturdays we take the children they do not swim much
but play and have fun

_____

_____

_____

_____

_____

_____

The Robin

Find the missing word in the story:

1. A _____ flew onto the ground next to Bill.

2. Bill flicked a _____ across to the robin.

3. The bird _____ at the nuts and seeds in the cake.

4. Lots of _____ were peeping through the soil.

5. "We need to weed between these _____," said Bill.

6. "Last year we grew _____ flowers here," said Bill.

7. "Gwen always _____ pink clothes," said Raf.

8. Meg ran into the _____ and the robin flew off.

9. Bill _____ the weeds onto the compost heap.

10. "I am going to get some _____ too," said Bill.

Find 2 words in the story for each spelling of the sound /oo/:

<oo>	<ew>	<ue>
_____	_____	_____
_____	_____	_____

Write a sentence for each word:

_____

_____

_____

_____

_____

_____

_____

_____

The Robin

1. Where was the robin?

   _____

2. Did the robin eat the worm?

   _____

3. Did the robin eat Liz's bird cake?

   _____

4. What month of the year was it?

   _____

5. What colour flowers will they be planting this year?

   _____

6. Why will Gwen be pleased?

   _____

7. Who was watching the robin on the wheelbarrow?

   _____

8. Where was the broom kept?

   _____

9. Where did Bill tip the weeds?

   _____

10. Why does the robin like the compost heap?

    _____

Practice reading and writing these words from the story:
Write each syllable and say the sounds as you go, then write the
whole word:

rob-in   _____ ____   _____   _____

litt-le   _____ ____   _____   _____

in-sect   ____ _____   _____   _____

com-post   _____ _____   _____   _____

af-ter-noon   ___ ___ _____   _____   _____

wheel-ba-rrow   _____ ___ _____   _____   _____

The Robin

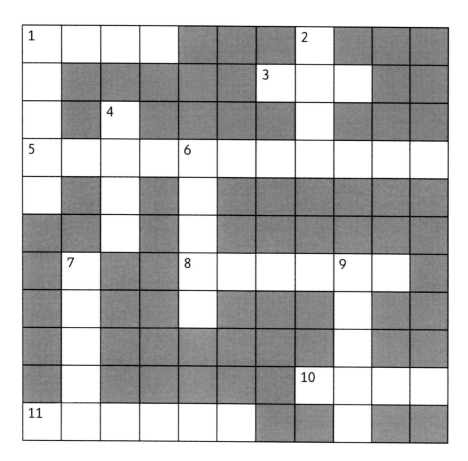

Across
1. Gwen's favourite colour (4)
3. The cat (3)
5. Used to collect weeds (11)
8. Fussy (6)
10. Stab at food with a beak (4)
11. It has 6 legs (6)

Down
1. Creep along (5)
2. 365 days (4)
4. Wild plant (4)
6. Meal at midday (5)
7. Bird with red breast (5)
9. Brush with a broom (5)

Choose 3 words and write a sentence for each:

_____

_____

_____

_____

_____

_____

_____

_____

_____

The Robin

Number these sentences in the order they appear in the story:

☐   Meg was prowling about.

☐   "This year I think we will have pink flowers," said Bill.

☐   Bill tipped the weeds onto the compost heap.

1   A robin flew onto the ground next to Bill.

☐   "It will be summer soon," said Bill to Raf.

☐   Bill flicked a worm to the robin.

Now write the sentences in the correct order:

1. _____

2. _____

3. _____

4. _____

5. _____

6. _____

Write about working in the garden. Think about:

1. Do you like gardening?

2. How big is your garden?

3. Who helps with the gardening?

4. What do you grow?

5. Do you have an allotment?

_____

_____

_____

_____

_____

Lite Bites

Find the missing word in the story:

1.   Liz decides to change the _____.

2.   "We must not have _____ on the menu all the time."

3.   Liz asks them what type of _____ they might like.

4.   "We need to eat food that is not high in _____ or fat."

5.   "I like _____ and rice best," says Ali.

6.   "Give me _____ and chips every time," says Ken.

7.   "All these things are not good for my _____," says Flick.

8.   "I can bring you lots of _____ fish," says Fred.

9.   "I will try and _____ a menu to suit everyone," says Liz.

10. "We can call them _____ Bites," says Liz.

Find 2 words in the story for each spelling of the sound /ie/:

<ie>	<igh>	<i>
_____	_____	_____
_____	_____	_____

Write a sentence for each word:

_____

_____

_____

_____

_____

_____

_____

_____

Lite Bites

1. What does Liz decide to do?
   _____

2. Why do Flick and Jess need lighter meals?
   _____

3. What food does the Slimming Club suggest?
   _____

4. What food does Ali like?
   _____

5. What does Frank like?
   _____

6. What food does Fred suggest?
   _____

7. What must you not have on baked potatoes?
   _____

8. Is soup good for you?
   _____

9. Will Liz still have pie and chips on the menu?
   _____

10. What will Liz call the new meals?
    _____

Practice reading and writing these words from the story:
Write each syllable and say the sounds as you go, then write the whole word:

di-et   _____ _____   _____   _____

men-u   _____ ____   _____   _____

tast-y   _____ _____   _____   _____

de-cide   ____ _____   _____   _____

i-de-as   ___ _____ _____   _____   _____

pot-a-toes   _____ ___ _____   _____   _____

Lite Bites

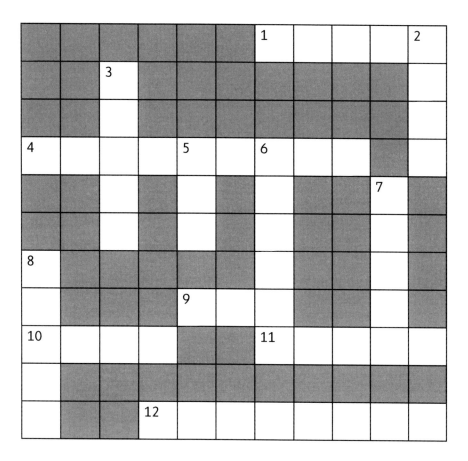

Across
1. Cooked in oil (5)
4. Plants that we eat (9)
9. Made with pastry (3)
10. Cooked grain (4)
11. Cook in the oven (5)
12. Losing weight (8)

Down
2. Dip into soup (4)
3. Used to make things sweet (5)
5. Attempt to do (3)
6. Made from milk (6)
7. Made from potatoes (5)
8. Hot Indian dish (5)

Choose 3 words and write a sentence for each:

_____

_____

_____

_____

_____

_____

_____

_____

_____

_____

Lite Bites

Number these sentences in the order they appear in the story:

☐ "I like curry and rice best," says Ali.

☐ "We will call them 'Lite Bites," says Liz.

☐ "Let's give Liz some ideas for lighter meals," says Flick.

☐ "Pie and chips for me!" says Frank.

[1] Liz decides to change the menu.

☐ "Roast vegetables are tasty," says Jess.

Now write the sentences in the correct order:

1. _____

2. _____

3. _____

4. _____

5. _____

6. _____

Write about your favourite food. Think about:

1. What food do you like?

2. Do you eat healthy food?

3. Do you ever go on a diet?

4. Have you ever been to a Slimming Club?

5. Do you like to eat out?

_____

_____

_____

_____

_____

The Football Match

Find the missing word in the story:

1. Most _____ the men go to a football match.

2. Last Saturday they met at the Drop-In at _____.

3. Sam _____ the van round to the front.

4. Flick had a bag full of _____ and crisps.

5. Flick _____ into the back of the van.

6. There were _____ of fans in the stadium.

7. There was a lot of shouting and _____.

8. Flick was shocked at some of the _____ in the songs.

9. They were _____ but happy.

10. "Could I come again?" asked _____.

Find 2 words in the story for each spelling of the sound /oo/:

<oo>   <u>   <oul>

_____   _____   _____

_____   _____   _____

Write a sentence for each word:

_____

_____

_____

_____

_____

_____

_____

_____

The Football Match

1. On what day do the men go to the football?

   _____

2. At what time did they meet at the Drop-In?

   _____

3. Who wanted to go with them?

   _____

4. What did Flick take with her?

   _____

5. At what time did the game start?

   _____

6. Why was Flick shocked when they were singing?

   _____

7. Did their team win the game?

   _____

8. Why did it take a long time to get out of the stadium?

   _____

9. Where did Flick put her empty bag?

   _____

10. Did Flick enjoy the game?

   _____

Practice reading and writing these words from the story:
Write each syllable and say the sounds as you go, then write the whole word:

emp-ty   _____ _____   _____   _____

hun-gry   _____ _____   _____   _____

some-times _____ _____   _____   _____

Sat-ur-day _____ ___ _____   _____   _____

stad-i-um _____ __ _____   _____   _____

ex-cit-ed _____ _____ _____   _____   _____

The Football Match

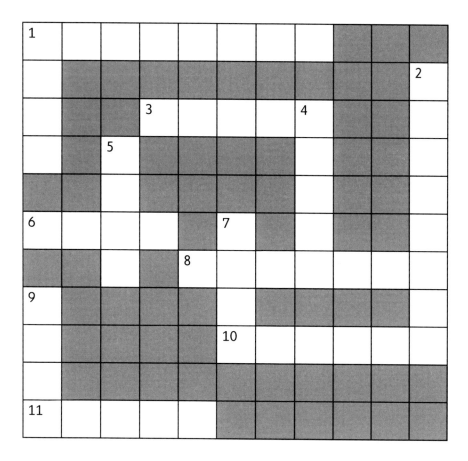

Across

1. A ball is kicked in this game (8)
3. Speak loudly (5)
6. Complain (4)
8. 100 (7)
10. In need of food (6)
11. Midday meal (5)

Down

1. Things we eat (4)
2. Day after Friday (8)
4. Needing to sleep (5)
5. Something to sit on (4)
7. Move something away (4)
9. No more room (4)

Choose 3 words and write a sentence for each:

_____

_____

_____

_____

_____

_____

_____

_____

_____

The Football Match

Number these sentences in the order they appear in the story:

☐   There are hundreds of fans in the stadium.

1   They all met at the Drop-In at 10 o'clock.

☐   "Make room for me – I've got the food!" said Flick.

☐   "You could come every time if you bring the lunch!" said Frank.

☐   There was a lot of shouting and singing.

☐   It took a long time to get back to the Drop-In.

Now write the sentences in the correct order:

1. _____

2. _____

3. _____

4. _____

5. _____

6. _____

Write about football. Think about:

1. Do you play football?

2. Do any of your family play football?

3. Do you watch football on TV?

4. Have you been to a match?

5. What other sports do you like?

_____

_____

_____

_____

_____

Race Night

Find the missing word in the story:

1. Every _____ Sam organises a Race Night.

2. Everyone watches horse races on a big _____.

3. This year Race Night was on _____.

4. Liz had bought _____ and beef burgers.

5. _____ made a big salad.

6. By _____ o'clock the food was ready in the fridge.

7. "Four is my lucky _____," said Dan.

8. "I will cheer for horse number _____," said Rima.

9. Horse number four came _____ in its race.

10. "Cheers Liz! Cheers Sam! Thanks for a great _____!"

Find a word in the story for each spelling for the sound /or/:

<or> _____   <aw> _____   <our> _____   <au> _____

Write a sentence for each word:

_____

_____

_____

_____

_____

_____

_____

_____

Race Night

1. In what month does Sam organise a Race Night?

    _____

2. What happens at a Race Night?

    _____

3. Who swept the patio and wiped down the tables?

    _____

4. What shape were the rolls for the beef burgers?

    _____

5. What did Fran make?

    _____

6. What did the fruit punch have in it?

    _____

7. Where was the big screen?

    _____

8. What is Ken's lucky number?

    _____

9. What was Rima's reward when her horse won the race?

    _____

10. Where did Ken's horse come in its race?

    _____

Practice reading and writing these words from the story:
Write each syllable and say the sounds as you go, then write the whole word:

ex-tra   _____ _____   _____   _____

num-ber   _____ _____   _____   _____

Au-gust   _____ _____   _____   _____

co-co-nut   ____ ____ _____   _____   _____

or-gan-ise   ____ _____ ____   _____   _____

Wed-nes-day   _____ ____ _____   _____   _____

Race Night

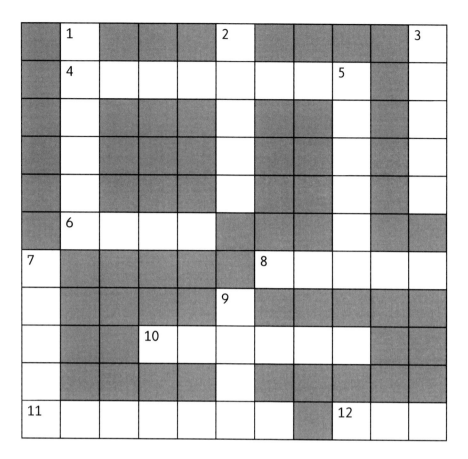

Across

4. Used to keep off the rain (8)
6. Competition to see who wins (4)
8. A bit more (5)
10. Pick something (6)
11. Time at the end of the day (7)
12. Give money to buy something (3)

Down

1. Meat eaten in a roll (6)
2. 7 (5)
3. Used for a cold drink (5)
5. Month after July (6)
7. A reward for the winner (5)
9. Come together (4)

Choose 3 words and write a sentence for each:

_____

_____

_____

_____

_____

_____

_____

_____

Race Night

Join the two parts of each sentence with a line:

Every August Sam organises   was ready in the fridge.

Liz bought sausages and   first in its race.

By four o'clock the food   beef burgers.

"I will cheer for horse number   a Race Night at the Drop-In.

Horse number four came   a great evening!"

"Thanks for   seven," said Rima.

Write the complete sentences:

_____

_____

_____

_____

_____

_____

_____

_____

Re-write this story adding the capital letters and full stops:

it was a hot summer evening in july pat and rob invited their friends for a bbq pat bought meat and made a salad rob cooked the meat on the bbq everyone had a great time

_____

_____

_____

_____

_____

_____

_____

The Fair

Find the missing word in the story:

1. Every _____ a fair comes to town.

2. "Where is the _____?" asks Rima.

3. "Wear warm _____," says Fran.

4. They meet at the Drop-In at _____.

5. They can see the glare of the _____.

6. "Sometimes it is good to be _____!" grins Gwen.

7. "I will have _____ now!" says Flick.

8. "Shall we go on the Swing _____ instead?" says Rima.

9. They look _____ when they stagger off!

10. Dan and Ken have a go at _____.

Find a word in the story for each spelling for the sound /or/:

\<are\> _____   \<air\> _____   \<ere\> _____   \<ear\> _____

Write a sentence for each word:

_____

_____

_____

_____

_____

_____

_____

_____

The Fair

1.   What comes to town every September?

   _____

2.   Has Rima ever been to a fair?

   _____

3.   Where is the fair set up?

   _____

4.   What does Frank suggest Rima should wear?

   _____

5.   At what time do they meet at the Drop-In?

   _____

6.   Why is it cheaper to go in the van?

   _____

7.   Why does Bill not hear the music?

   _____

8.   What ride do Frank and Flick go on?

   _____

9.   Why do Ali and Chang feel sick?

   _____

10.   Why does Dan win a cuddly bear?

   _____

Practice reading and writing these words from the story:
Write each syllable and say the sounds as you go, then write the
whole word:

pet-rol   _____ _____   _____   _____

ex-cept   ____ _____   _____   _____

night-mare   _____ _____   _____   _____

Sep-tem-ber   ____ ____ ____   _____   _____

un-der-wear   ____ ____ _____   _____   _____

diff-er-ent   ____ ____ _____   _____   _____

The Fair

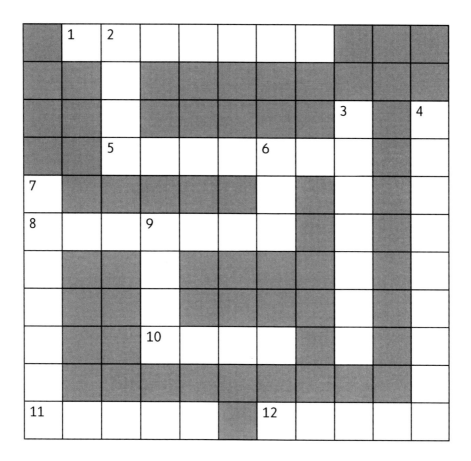

Across
1. Month after September (7)
5. Material that keeps in body heat (7)
8. 100 (7)
10. Cost of a journey (4)
11. Water flowing to the sea (5)
12. Not day (5)

Down
2. Amount to pay (4)
3. Things we wear (7)
4. Not the same (9)
6. Soil mixed with water (3)
7. Costing less (7)
9. Not able to hear (4)

Choose 3 words and write a sentence for each:

_____

_____

_____

_____

_____

_____

_____

_____

The Fair

Join the two parts of each sentence with a line:

Every September   the cost of the petrol.

It is set up on   Swing Boats, instead?"

We can share   a fair comes to town.

"I dare you   and won a cuddly bear!"

"Shall we go on the   the field next to the river.

"I shot all the cans down   to go on the Ghost Train."

Write the complete sentences:

_____

_____

_____

_____

_____

_____

_____

_____

_____

Re-write this story adding the capital letters and full stops:

"hello! my name is bert i have a fair we travel from place to place we set
up our rides and stalls and stay in each place for a week"
people love it when bert's fair comes to town

_____

_____

_____

_____

_____

_____

The Farm

Find the missing word in the story:

1. "Let's visit _____ _____," said Sam.

2. Charlie Dance was at _____ with Sam.

3. The next _____ they met at the Drop-In at 10am.

4. "I can take my car," said _____.

5. Archie, the _____, barked and jumped up.

6. They passed _____ leaning out of his stable door.

7. They went over the _____ and past a field of cows.

8. The _____ were running and jumping about.

9. Scott bought an _____ cake made by Mrs Dance.

10. "Maybe I will have _____ a piece," said Flick.

Find 2 words in the story for each spelling of the sound /ar/:

<ar>	<a>	<al>
_____	_____	_____
_____	_____	_____

Write a sentence for each word:

_____

_____

_____

_____

_____

_____

_____

_____

The Farm

1. Why is it called Dance Farm?

   _____

2. Who offered to take his car?

   _____

3. Where did Sam park the van?

   _____

4. What was the sheepdog called?

   _____

5. What did they see curled up with Sparkle?

   _____

6. Why was the horse called Star?

   _____

7. What did Bill think Emma said?

   _____

8. What were the lambs doing?

   _____

9. What did Liz buy in the farm shop?

   _____

10. How much fudge did Flick and Jess have?

    _____

Practice reading and writing these words from the story:
Write each syllable and say the sounds as you go, then write the
whole word:

vis-it   _____ _____   _____   _____

sta-ble   _____ _____   _____   _____

corn-er   _____ _____   _____   _____

danc-ing   _____ _____   _____   _____

sheep-dog   _____ _____   _____   _____

an-i-mals   ____ __ _____   _____   _____

The Farm

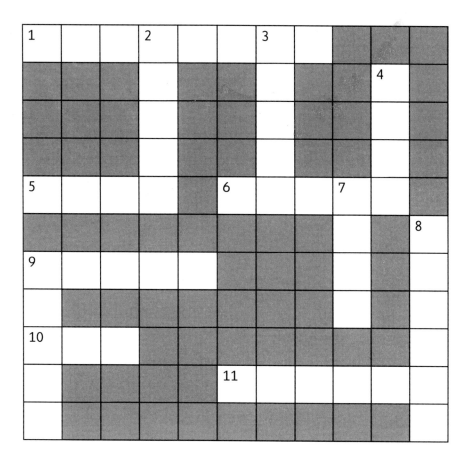

Across
1. Hard area on a farm (8)
5. Used to sit in and wash (4)
6. Rough path (5)
9. We get wool from them (5)
10. Belonging to (3)
11. Home for a horse (6)

Down
2. Boggy land by a river (5)
3. Water flowing to the sea (5)
4. Not front (4)
7. Baby cow (4)
8. Baby cat (6)
9. Speak loudly (5)

Choose 3 words and write a sentence for each:

_____

_____

_____

_____

_____

_____

_____

_____

The Farm

Join the two parts of each sentence with a line:

Dance Farm is owned	with a white mark on his nose.
Sam parked the van	of cheese and some milk.
Star was dark brown	by Charlie Dance.
They went over the bridge	proud of us!"
Liz bought a large piece	next to an old tin bath.
"Slimming Club would be	and past a field of cows.

Write the complete sentences:

_____

_____

_____

_____

_____

_____

_____

_____

_____

Re-write this story adding the capital letters and full stops:

oxley farm is owned by george and daisy oxley they have cows, sheep and pigs george milks the cows twice a day daisy makes cheese and sells it in the shop vera comes in to help in the shop during july and august when they have lots of visitors to the farm

_____

_____

_____

_____

_____

BLUEPRINT

Topics

Jim Fitzsimmons

Rhona Whiteford

Stanley Thornes (Publishers) Ltd

First published in 1989 by
Stanley Thornes (Publishers) Ltd
Old Station Drive
Leckhampton
CHELTENHAM GL53 0DN

Reprinted 1990
Reprinted 1991

British Library Cataloguing in Publication Data

Fitzsimmons, Jim
    Topics. — (Blueprints).
    I. Great Britain. Primary schools.
    Curriculum: Topics
    I. Title   II. Whiteford, Rhona   III. Series
    372.19
    ISBN 0-7487-0091-9

Typeset by Tech-Set, Gateshead, Tyne & Wear.
Printed in Great Britain at The Bath Press, Avon.

CONTENTS

INTRODUCTION

Blueprints: Topics is a teacher resource book that provides a wealth of practical ideas and 70 photocopiable sheets on common key topics for the 5 to 8 age group. All the topics are cross-referenced to National Curriculum core subject attainment targets to help with your curriculum planning. For each of the 10 topics the book provides the following resources:

- a topic web mapping out the topic across the curriculum and giving attainment targets for core subjects;
- a list of basic concepts that the topic introduces;
- practical activities related to the topic web for each subject area;
- photocopiable activity sheets for pupil use. These can form the basis of individual topic books or classroom displays.

It has long been thought that an interdisciplinary approach to topic work gives a more holistic view for the child and encourages more effective learning. With this in mind, the topics in this book have been designed to be cross-curricular and contain all the elements of the National Curriculum's core and foundation subjects, relevant to the particular age groups.

The topics are loosely graded at three levels of difficulty to meet the needs of the first three years of school. Loosely, the first three topics are for reception classes, the second three for middle infants and the final four for top infants and first year juniors. The ideas for work in each topic are designed to fit in with general expectations of attainment for the age group, and are based on the authors' wide experience of teaching these age groups. However, the topics do represent a continuum of difficulty and no attempt has been made formally to grade them; you will find that they can be fitted to the needs of your own individual situation and children.

Blueprints: Topics provides ideas for approaching topics from many different angles and allows the teacher and children to choose their own starting points. It does not attempt to replace the many excellent individual subject topic books available, but is designed to help the teacher to plan an overall strategy. This means that the topics may be studied in their entirety or single subject areas may be studied in isolation. The cross-curricular references are available when required to enable you to integrate the topics into your National Curriculum planning.

Other books in this series include *Blueprints: Writing* and *Blueprints: Assemblies*. Many of the ideas, activities and photocopiable pages in these books can be used to complement the topics in this book.

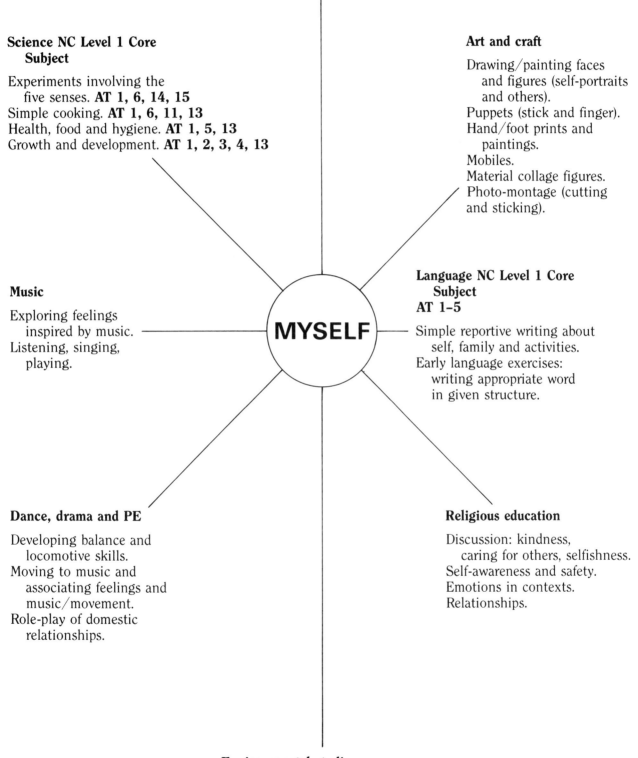

Mathematics NC Level 1 Core Subject

Measurement of body-parts:
    length of stride, height,
    hand size, etc. **AT 1, 8, 9**
Comparisons and differences,
    e.g. hair/skin/eye colour. **AT 12**
Simple graph and charts. **AT 13**

Science NC Level 1 Core Subject

Experiments involving the
    five senses. **AT 1, 6, 14, 15**
Simple cooking. **AT 1, 6, 11, 13**
Health, food and hygiene. **AT 1, 5, 13**
Growth and development. **AT 1, 2, 3, 4, 13**

Art and craft

Drawing/painting faces
    and figures (self-portraits
    and others).
Puppets (stick and finger).
Hand/foot prints and
    paintings.
Mobiles.
Material collage figures.
Photo-montage (cutting
    and sticking).

Music

Exploring feelings
    inspired by music.
Listening, singing,
    playing.

MYSELF

Language NC Level 1 Core Subject AT 1–5

Simple reportive writing about
    self, family and activities.
Early language exercises:
    writing appropriate word
    in given structure.

Dance, drama and PE

Developing balance and
    locomotive skills.
Moving to music and
    associating feelings and
    music/movement.
Role-play of domestic
    relationships.

Religious education

Discussion: kindness,
    caring for others, selfishness.
Self-awareness and safety.
Emotions in contexts.
Relationships.

Environmental studies

Exploration of local environment,
    recording important features.

1

MYSELF

1 You are alive. You breathe; your heart beats; you have blood.
2 You are a human. Humans have different skin and hair colours.
3 You need water, food and warmth to live.
4 You need love and companionship too.
5 Humans have to learn to live together in peace and harmony.
6 You learn about the world you live in by using your five senses: sight, touch, taste, hearing and smell.

STARTING POINT

Children can bring in photographs of themselves as babies and at various stages in their development. They could also bring in items for a small display: baby clothes and shoes, Christening gifts, favourite toys, recent birthday cards, etc.

If possible, invite a parent to bring a baby or toddler into school and let the class observe the size of body parts: fingers, feet, head, neck, and so on. The children could discuss with the mother and their teacher what skills the baby has, and compare the baby's stage of development with their own. How have they progressed? If appropriate, talk about pregnancy and birth, growth and change.

LANGUAGE

The language exercises recommended here are suitable for use towards the end of the reception year, or once the children have grasped the basic concepts of sentence construction and have progressed well in reading. As an aid to writing, you could display a poster with all the basic vocabulary for the different parts of the body.

MYSELF 1: This is me

Each child can write his or her name on the flag, add details to the figure and then colour it so that it represents himself or herself. In the space below, the child can write simple sentences such as:

My name is . . .
I live in . . .
I play with . . .

I have a pet. . . .
I am a boy/girl.
I go to school in . . .

MYSELF 2: My Mum/My Dad

You can make two pages from this page, or – for children from one-parent families – use just one half. To use the top half, cover the bottom half with plain paper before photocopying. You will thus create a space where the child can add extra information about his/her parent. To use the bottom half, move the book so that this half now becomes the top part of the page, position a piece of plain paper to form the bottom part of the page, and then photocopy.

The children add details to the figures – hair, skin colour, etc. – and can alter the clothes as they wish. Then they fill in Mum's/Dad's name and add whatever other information they like in the space available.

MYSELF 3: My family

Inside the outline of the house the children draw all the members of their family, including pets if they wish. They write each name under the appropriate picture, and then, if possible, write a sentence about who lives in their house. Additional writing on a separate sheet could be about: Helping Mummy or Daddy; My baby brother or sister; The most exciting day; My favourite toy; or Things I like (e.g. food, TV programme, game).

MATHEMATICS

Much valuable language development can be derived from comparisons of different parts of the body: height, length of arms and legs, stride, reach. These comparisons can be recorded in a visually pleasing way by taking the measurements with strips of brightly coloured crepe paper and producing a simple chart to show tallest/longest to shortest. Language is basic to the understanding of mathematics, so this type of activity is valuable in the early stages. It also enables children to see themselves in relation to others, e.g. I am taller than David and shorter than Susan. For a really striking comparison, take a very large sheet of paper and draw around your foot, the largest child's foot and the smallest child's foot. Use the result as the base for a vocabulary chart on which to display words like *longer, shorter, longest, shortest, tall, short, taller, tallest, big, small, large, wide, narrow.*

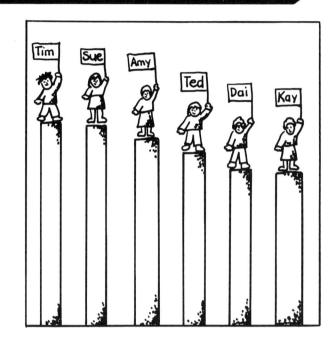

MYSELF 4: Mitten and shoes

You can either use this as one sheet, or make two pages of it as described for sheet 2: My Mum/My Dad.

Inside the mitten the child can draw around his or her own hand. This will provide an exercise in manual control and dexterity and give the child a personal record of hand size, for comparison with others. The word 'hand' goes in the box provided.

The 'shoe' exercise is self-explanatory.

MYSELF 5: All about me

This is a checklist of personal information which the child completes with words and with pictures of himself or herself, a friend, his/her home, a pet and a favourite toy.

Here are some simple experiments to help the children identify and discuss their senses.

Touch

Make a 'feely box' – a box with a hole in each end, covered with a cloth so that the children cannot see inside. Place various common objects, *one at a time*, inside the box. Use coins, cotton reels, a comb, a spoon and small toys; or a collection of different flat shapes. Let the children take turns to feel inside the box and make a guess about the identity of the object.

This activity can be more demanding if you ask the children to grade sandpaper as coarse, medium, fine and extra fine (the children can simply say 'roughest, next roughest, smooth and smoothest'). In order to establish the idea of texture, cover a board with squares of different materials, or make a collage of a clown or toy using different materials. Allow the children to touch freely and discuss their thoughts.

Taste and smell

Collect a range of things which have a strong smell, e.g. coffee, fish-paste, mothballs, vinegar, cheese, apple, orange, banana. Put each in a small container with a tissue over the top and let the children take turns to sniff as you lift the edge of the tissue.

Then collect a range of things to taste, such as carrot, banana, crisps, apple, grapes and chocolate. Cut the foods into small pieces, and make the children close their eyes (or blindfold them) before they taste. Then ask the children to taste some of the foods while they hold their noses, and see if the results are the same.

Hearing

Make a collection of objects which will make a noise, e.g. a bell, cup and saucer, key, tambourine, triangle, glass and spoon, typewriter. Let the children work in small groups. One group at a time, let them first experiment with the objects and discuss the sounds they make, then ask them to sit with their backs to the objects and identify the sounds you make. Vary this by making a recording of household noises, e.g. a door closing, a doorbell, a pan clanging, water running, a sewing machine, a vacuum cleaner, an electric mixer, etc. To record the activities you could make a class display of two sets of things: those the children identified by sound and those they could not identify. Use pictures cut from magazines for the display.

Sight

Let the children try these simple experiments to show that our eyes can play tricks on us. Work with small groups and keep the language very simple.

1 Hold both forefingers nail to nail about 6 cm in front of the eyes. Look at an imaginary point *just beyond them*, but do not look directly at the fingers. If the fingers are separated slowly, this is what can be seen.

2 Roll up a piece of card to make a 3 cm tube and look through the tube at anything in the room. Cover the other eye with your hand and keep both eyes open. Slowly move your hand away from your eye along the side of the tube, and this illusion will be seen.

3 Draw the picture below on a piece of card and ask the children in turn if they see a candlestick or two faces staring at each other. To check each answer, ask the child to point out where the candle would go (if necessary have another drawing available of a candle in the candlestick) or where the noses are on the faces and where the eyes would go.

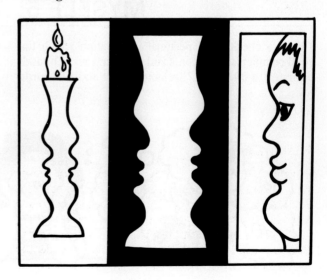

4 Draw lines like this on a piece of card and ask the children to point to the longest line. Have a piece of card cut to the exact length of the lines, to use as a measure to prove they are all the same length.

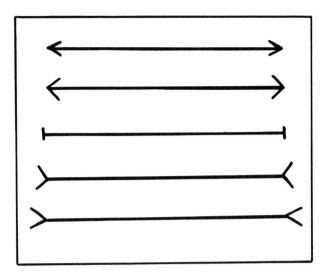

This simple test will help to show how much we need our eyes ... Chalk a straight line about 3 m long on the playground. Blindfold the children one at a time and ask them to walk along the line. Mark each child's pathway with chalk and write his or her name at the end. Then you can see who has walked the straightest line.

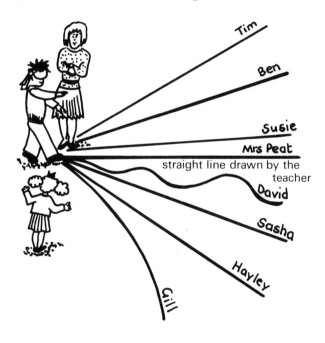

straight line drawn by the teacher

Health and hygiene

Bring in a variety of foods with a wide range of nutritional values. Make sure you have examples of foods that all the ethnic groups in school eat. Try to put the foods into sets as you discuss them with the children: those that are good for healthy teeth; those which give us energy; those that help make us grow. On the negative side, identify those foods which, when eaten to excess, make us overweight and unwell, e.g. an excess of fatty foods can lead to heart disease. Make a set of foods which contain a lot of fat. Stress that we need a little of each type of food each day, but not too much of any.

Write to one of the big toothpaste manufacturers, who usually supply free wallcharts and samples of toothpaste and brushes. You can then arrange for the children to bring in their own toothbrushes so that they can brush their teeth at school. Establish good hygiene habits as part of your daily routine, e.g. washing hands before meals and after messy work and the handling of pets; and encourage the children to think about their appearance. If you provide toothbrushes, towels, sponges, etc. in the home corner, the children can consolidate their learning by looking after the dolls.

Talk about the importance of exercise for good health. Children need vigorous daily exercise to help develop good heart muscles, so try to include some PE each day, even if it's only races outdoors (for which there is no need for PE kit).

Make some sweets

Make a stiff icing and add one teaspoon of glycerine to each cupful of icing. Then add food colourings and flavourings, but try unusual combinations, e.g. red colour and lemon flavour; green colour and strawberry flavour. Sprinkle icing sugar onto a board for shaping the sweets. Make small balls of icing and flatten each with the palm. Let them dry until they are easy to lift, and then place them into sweet cases. The sweets could be dipped into melted chocolate for added interest. Don't forget to make children aware of the dangers of cookers, hot water and hot melted chocolate as you work. Good behaviour at times like this is an important lesson in self-control and awareness, as children learn to become more responsible for their own safety.

A discussion about the dangers of eating strange things could be included here. Bring in examples of common berries and fungi from garden and field and stress to children that they should not eat anything they are not sure of, because they could be poisoned or made ill. Your school may have its own policy about dangerous drugs, and the advisability of mentioning the dangers of inhaling fumes (i.e. glue-sniffing) to very young children.

Faces

The children could paint self-portraits which can be mounted as a class 'photograph' or hung as mobiles, with each child's name clearly showing.

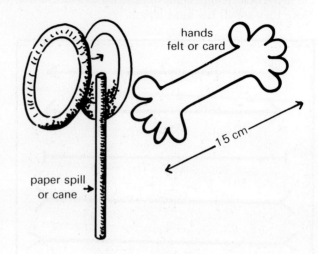

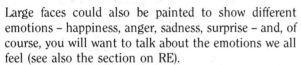

Large faces could also be painted to show different emotions – happiness, anger, sadness, surprise – and, of course, you will want to talk about the emotions we all feel (see also the section on RE).

Paper-plate puppet

You will need two paper plates, one piece of activity paper, glue, scissors, paints or crayons, wool, scraps of material and a large piece of lightweight material or crepe paper (25 cm by 50 cm), pipe-cleaners, and felt or card for the hands. Roll the activity paper into a tight spill and staple it to the front of one of the plates. Glue the front of the second plate to the front of the first one, to form the head. Add features with paint, felt-pen or crayon, with perhaps a button or a milk-bottle top for the nose. Using wool or felt, add the hair.

Gather the material or crepe paper for the skirt around the neck-end of the spill, and fix it with a pipe-cleaner. Make sure the open ends of the skirt are at the back. If you use material, it must be very light or the head will bend; if necessary a garden cane can be used instead of a paper spill. Finally, staple or stick the hands to the back of the neck, and add a ribbon if you like. For boys, pretend the 'dress' is a shirt. Paint buttons down the front and add a tie instead of a ribbon.

Printing

To develop body awareness, use hands and fingers, and possibly feet, to print with paint. Children can help with the cutting out.

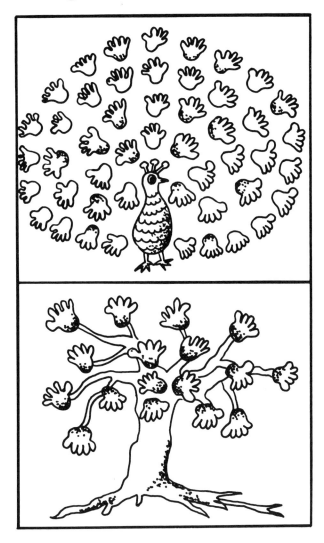

Jellyfish mobiles

Print hand shapes and cut them out. Decorate them with sticky-paper eyes, nose and mouth and suspend them in groups from the ceiling, using crepe-paper or Cellophane® strips. Add Cellophane® seaweed fronds.

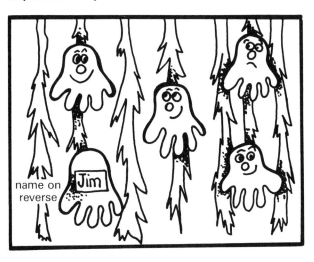

Finger-print flowers

Print onto ready-cut flower shapes, using fingers or thumbs dipped directly into the paint. The flowers can be displayed in large plant-pots with stems and leaves cut from activity paper.

7

Finger puppets

Cut the two finger shapes approximately 4 cm by 8 cm and glue the edges together. The children can be helped to do this carefully. The finger can then be decorated in whatever way desired by gluing on scraps of felt, braid, beads, buttons, etc.

Photo-montage

Let the children practise their cutting out by collecting arms, legs, heads, eyes, mouths or whole bodies from catalogues and magazines. These can then be stuck onto paper shapes as montage sets of eyes, mouths, etc. An amusing variation would be to make a composite picture of 'strange people'.

![MUSIC](music banner)

Music can affect the way we feel. Play different types of music to the children and discuss how each makes them feel: strong, happy, sad, sleepy, lively. Listen to music for different occasions, e.g. dancing, marching, Christmas, weddings, funerals. How do TV and other theme tunes make us feel, e.g. the themes from *Jaws*, *Barnum*, or children's TV? Sing a selection of songs and let the children experiment with non-tuned percussion instruments to try to create moods or ideas, e.g. a giant stamping through the house, a little mouse running across the table.

DANCE, DRAMA AND PE

The children can explore the space around their bodies by stretching and curling to make wide and narrow shapes. They can be shown how to use space effectively by using eyes and body control in simple exercises like stopping and restarting while running and walking. They can explore the limitations of their bodies by finding out how high they can jump, how wide they can stretch, how long they can balance on one leg, and so on.

Use different types of music to suggest different actions: slow music for smooth, graceful movements on the spot; irregular electronic music for jerky, robotic movements; exciting, fluid music for happy leaping and prancing. You can play various rhythms yourself using non-tuned percussion instruments or the piano.

In the home corner the children can try out the different roles in the family situation and begin to come to terms with their own position by feeling what it is like to be Mum or Dad or the baby again.

MYSELF 6: Things I can do

This is a checklist of personal skills. Children tick and colour in pictures of the various skills they have acquired to date. This should promote much discussion between the children as well as with you.

RELIGIOUS EDUCATION

Talk about moral issues appropriate to children of this age, e.g. sharing, selfishness, caring, helping, telling lies, stealing, etc. Illustrate the talks with well-known stories such as *Teddy Robinson* or *Postman Pat*. Talk about how the children see themselves: their role in the family or school, their abilities and skills, their shortcomings as identified by the adults in their lives. Talk about their fears, likes and dislikes; about the people who look after the children and keep them safe; and about the child's contribution to his or her own safety, for example, saying 'No' to strangers and keeping safe on the road. You can then discuss the rules which help us to live happily and safely together, e.g. the green cross code, school rules. All of this should contribute to each child's self-awareness and growing independence.

ENVIRONMENTAL STUDIES

Children's own histories can be explored through the photographs and objects they have brought in for the class display. Take care not to pry too deeply into any child's background unless he or she is willing.

A walk round the environs of school will be useful. Look for the different types of shops, offices, factories, homes, roads, railways, areas of water, parks and gardens, fields. When you return to school, each child could paint one feature and, with the help of an adult, cut it out and mount it on a frieze or a large picture of the neighbourhood. Children could each draw a picture of their own home so that it can be put on the frieze near its point of reference, e.g. Liz lives near the gas works; Andy lives near the farm.

MYSELF 7: Elements of a graph

Following discussion on individual and racial differences in skin, eye and hair colour, make a picture graph to illustrate the range within the class. Cut up enough photocopied sheets to give a set of features (eyes, hands and a face) to each child. The child colours the pictures to match his or her own features, thus providing personal data for the class picture.

9

This is me

Myself 1

My Mum

She is called

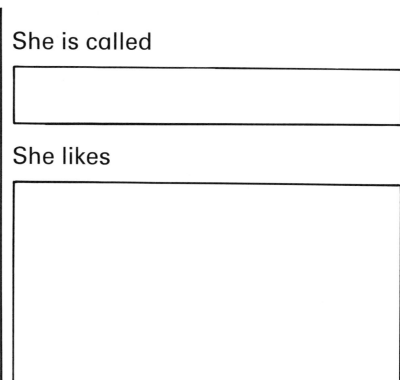

She likes

My Dad

He is called

He likes

Myself 2

11

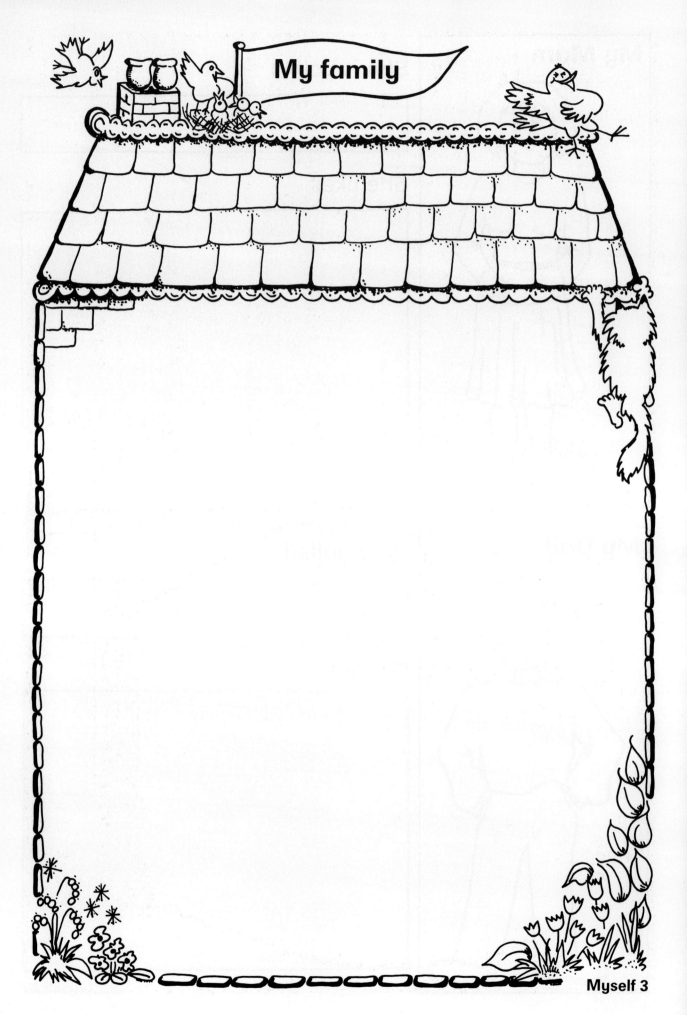

My family

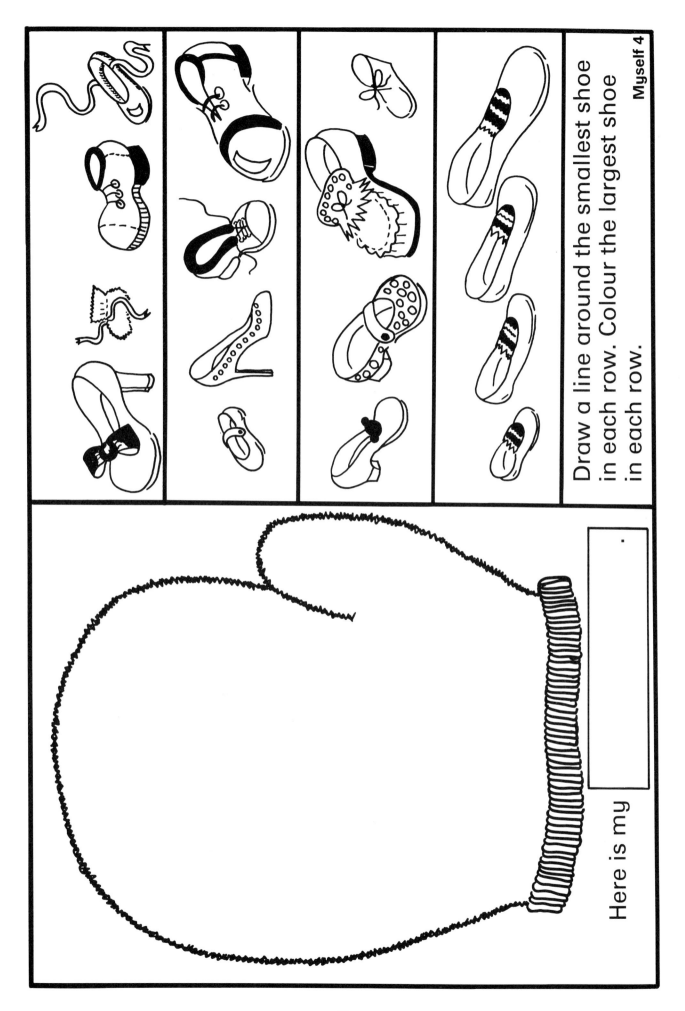

Draw a line around the smallest shoe in each row. Colour the largest shoe in each row.

Here is my

All about me

My name is [_____] .

I am [_____] years old.

I am a [_____] .   or

My hair is [_____] .

My eyes are [_____] .

This is me	My home	My friend
	A pet I would like	My favourite toy

Things I can do

run

jump

hop

skip

skip with a rope

ride a bike

balance on one leg

forward roll

swim

throw a ball

catch a ball

bat a ball

Myself 6

15

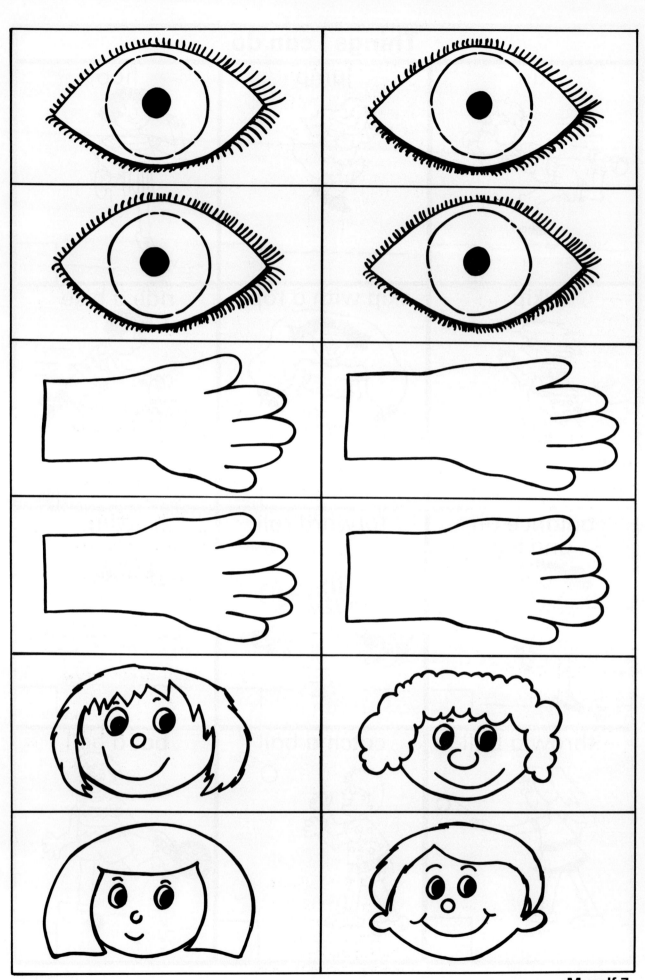

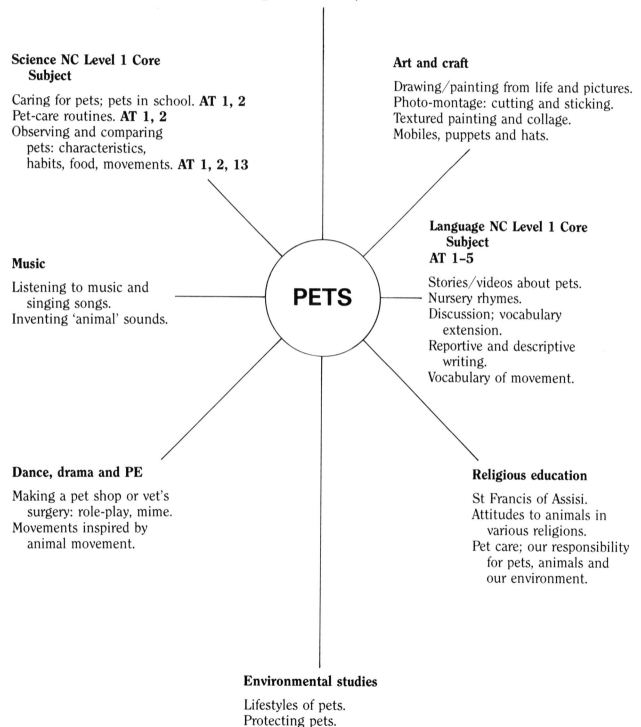

Mathematics NC Level 1 Core Subject

Sorting and classifying; matching. **AT 1, 2**
Time intervals in pet-care routines. **AT 8, 9**
Record keeping. **AT 13**
Measurement (non-standard units). **AT 8, 9**
Pictogram of pet ownership. **AT 13**
Ordering for size. **AT 8, 9**

Science NC Level 1 Core Subject

Caring for pets; pets in school. **AT 1, 2**
Pet-care routines. **AT 1, 2**
Observing and comparing pets: characteristics, habits, food, movements. **AT 1, 2, 13**

Art and craft

Drawing/painting from life and pictures.
Photo-montage: cutting and sticking.
Textured painting and collage.
Mobiles, puppets and hats.

Music

Listening to music and singing songs.
Inventing 'animal' sounds.

PETS

Language NC Level 1 Core Subject AT 1–5

Stories/videos about pets.
Nursery rhymes.
Discussion; vocabulary extension.
Reportive and descriptive writing.
Vocabulary of movement.

Dance, drama and PE

Making a pet shop or vet's surgery: role-play, mime.
Movements inspired by animal movement.

Religious education

St Francis of Assisi.
Attitudes to animals in various religions.
Pet care; our responsibility for pets, animals and our environment.

Environmental studies

Lifestyles of pets.
Protecting pets.
Hygiene and safety.
Working animals.
Animals in entertainment.

PETS

BASIC CONCEPTS

1 Pets are animals we share our lives with.

2 Pets are alive like us, and need love, care and companionship.

3 They need their own special food and place to live.

4 Many pets need exercise and some can be trained to do things.

5 Some pets can do jobs.

6 If a pet is injured or ill we must take it to the vet for help.

STARTING POINT

Children can bring in pictures and posters of different pets. These can be used as the backdrop for a display, which can include some of the foods and the utensils used for feeding and caring for pets. Add a few toy pets and use this display to encourage discussion of the difference between toys and live pets. For reference, see the DES regulations and your own LEA regulations about keeping pets in school. There is also an RSPCA handbook about each common pet, and these books are well laid out and colourful.

If you are going to keep any animal in school, even for a short time, ensure that conditions are as favourable as possible, both for the animal's sake and as a teaching point. Choose a school pet carefully, after consulting reference materials and seeking advice. Remember, too, that regulations may apply even to visiting animals; and that pets which owners know to be usually calm and well behaved may act out of character when faced with a large group of children. Cats and dogs are particularly unpredictable in the presence of young children.

Watch videos such as *The Aristocats, Lady and The Tramp, One Hundred and One Dalmations, Paddington Bear*, and some of the natural history tapes that are available now. Stories could include *Olga de Polga*; the *Paddington Bear* collections; *Mog the Cat*; and the *Postman Pat* series, which feature Jess, the cat.

Large posters of pets are available from the RSPCA.

LANGUAGE

Talk about the animals we normally consider as pets, and their qualities. Talk about the children's own pets, pets that have visited school, pets they would like to have, etc. Get the children to each draw and write a short description of a pet they would like to have. They could also write a reportive piece about general care of pets. If possible, ensure the children have some experience of this first, even if only for a day – they should observe how the animal behaved when feeding, playing and resting.

PETS 1: A pet shop

Children colour the picture and use the bottom part of the sheet for any of the writing suggested above.

18

PETS 2: Pets and petfoods

This is a simple matching activity which, when backed up by discussion, will tell the children quite a lot about some animals' feeding habits, needs and lifestyles.

PETS 3: Sleepy pets

Here matching is combined with tracking (a useful hand control exercise). Like us, pets need their own 'place' where they can go to sleep in safety, for example fish need rock crevices and weed where they can lie and hide.

MATHEMATICS

If you keep an animal in school, the daily feeding routine can provide opportunities for 'mathematical' conversations: the number of carrots the guinea pig eats each day; how many scoops of food for the rabbit; how many cupfuls of water in the bowl; when does the animal need feeding or cleaning or grooming (e.g. daily, twice a day, once a week).

PETS 4: Feeding pets

This record sheet offers a rather more structured approach to the activity mentioned above. For purposes of comparison, you need two school pets, or the school pet and a visiting pet, available for observation over a 7-day period. However, the activity can be carried out quite satisfactorily with a single animal.

Each child can have a copy of the sheet, or use just one copy, enlarged to A3, in a discussion situation. First the pet is drawn, if possible from life, and the information about type and age is filled in (obviously these are important facts when related to food consumption).

Where appropriate, use non-standard units of measure:

the same ones each day and for both (or all) the pets, so that comparisons are possible. Variations may be so wide, and the variables so numerous, that you will have to help the children to make and understand the comparisons. In some cases, diets may be so different as to render comparison meaningless.

Help the children to observe and record the daily intake carefully, over a one-week period. You will probably have to record the weekend feeds yourself, or ask whoever is responsible to do so for you. Stress the importance of regular feeding *every* day, weekends and holidays included.

PETS 5: Pictogram graph

You can organise a class pictogram showing which pets the children own or, alternatively, which pets they would like to own. Photocopy and cut up one sheet per child. Those pictures left over from the pictogram can be coloured by the children and stuck onto large sheets of paper in sets:

animals that have fur/animals that don't have fur;
animals that eat meat/animals that don't eat meat;
animals that have claws/animals that don't have claws.

The value of keeping pets in school lies in the opportunity it offers for close observation of other life forms. Stress that pets are alive like us and have the same needs for food, water, shelter, companionship and, at times, privacy. The only experiment which is harmless to the animal and comprehensible to this age group is testing to see what food the animal likes or dislikes. Generally animals do not eat food which is unsuitable, i.e. a budgie will not eat meat, yet dogs eat almost anything, depending on the individual. It is inadvisable to leave food in a water-based environment as this will contaminate the water. Similarly, if a caged pet does not accept the food left in the morning, the food should be thrown away for the sake of hygiene.

The children should be taught correct husbandry procedures and *careful* handling, although young children should never be left alone with pets. Furthermore, insist on the children washing their hands after handling the animals.

Observation and discussion are most valuable. Find out how old the animal is, and its life expectancy, and encourage the children to ask questions: *How does the animal move? Has it got ears, eyes, nose, mouth, legs, toes, tail? Where are its eyes positioned? What is its skin covered with (scales, fur, feathers)? What colour is it? How big is it compared to the children?*

ART AND CRAFT

Drawing, montage and painting

Pets can be drawn either from direct observation or from pictures or photographs. Cutting animal pictures from magazines will improve children's coordination skills and make them more adept with scissors; and the pictures can be mounted as a photo-montage. Let the children paint from life, if possible. The results could be mounted for use in the class 'pet shop' (see section on Drama).

Bird and fish mobiles

For the bird mobile, cut out basic bird shapes and decorate them on both sides (finger painting; sterile feathers; or paper feathers, cut and fringed). The wings

are made by folding a piece of paper like a concertina and pushing it through a slit in the body. The whole thing can be hung from the ceiling by a strip of crepe paper.

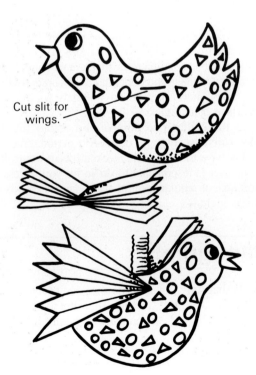

Cut slit for wings.

Display as a mobile with paper clouds.

Paper feet may be added.

For the fish mobile, decorate basic fish shapes as desired and add long fins and a tail made of cellophane or tissue. Suspend the fish from the ceiling in groups; or hang them against a wall inside a 'tank' made of strips of corrugated card stapled to the wall. Hang crepe and Cellophane® weeds around the fish.

Printed mobiles

Cut out different pet shapes from activity paper and print on them, using a variety of objects. Print some shapes on one side and some on the other, so that pairs can be glued or stapled together for rigidity, at the same time 'trapping' the end of a crepe strip from which the shape can be suspended.

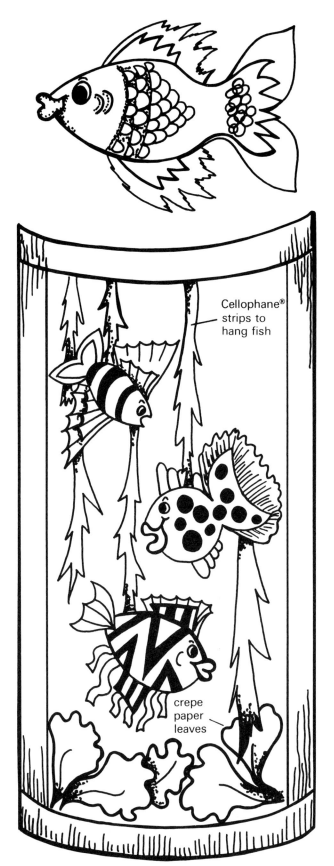

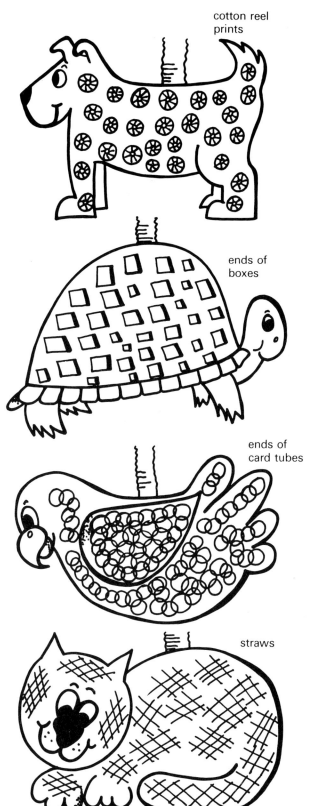

cotton reel prints

ends of boxes

ends of card tubes

straws

Textured painting

Mix PVA glue and poster paint to a thick consistency, and paint pet shapes. Using fingers or combs, the children can create interesting textures to represent different animal skins. Baskets can be painted too, with the weave 'combed' in; or hutches with textured 'wooden' sides.

Collage

Make a large collage – 'the pet show' – with different animals in suitable textured material: fur fabric or tangled wool for guinea pigs, milk-bottle tops for fish scales, wood shavings or feathers for birds, lamé for reptiles and snakes.

Puppets

Cut out two fish shapes and decorate them on opposite sides with shiny material. Glue both shapes together, enclosing the end of an activity-paper spill or a garden cane. Other puppets can include tortoise, rabbit, monkey, mouse and guinea pig. The monkey and rabbit can have long limbs made from pieces of paper folded like a concertina; and heads and bodies formed from paper plates, painted appropriately.

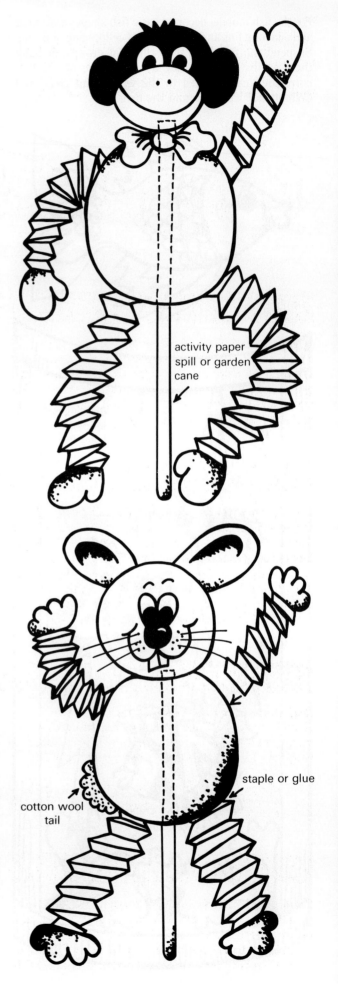

activity paper spill or garden cane

cotton wool tail

staple or glue

Hats

These are simply decorated shapes attached to card headbands. Most pet shapes can be used. Talk to the children about different characteristics like size of ears, whiskers, noses, eye position, teeth and shape of face.

Fold out slightly.

MUSIC

Listen to *Carnival of Animals* by Saint-Saëns and *Peter and the Wolf* by Prokofiev. Discuss why particular sounds are used to represent particular animals. Using any instruments you have available, try to invent sounds that represent animal movements, e.g. 'These bells are a bird pecking very quickly at its seed.'

Sing songs and nursery rhymes: 'Hickory, Dickory, Dock'; 'Daddy Wouldn't Buy Me a Bow-wow'; 'I Love Little Pussy'; 'Oh Where, Oh Where has my Little Dog gone?'; 'How Much is that Doggie in the Window?'

DANCE, DRAMA AND PE

Turn the home corner into a pet shop, using stuffed toys as pets and large cardboard boxes as cages. Discuss the need to keep certain animals apart. Ask the children to bring in empty, clean petfood containers, use polystyrene chips as corn and flour-and-water dough to make dog biscuits, which can be baked and varnished. Children can pretend to be pets if the boxes are large enough.

You could make a veterinary surgery instead of a pet

shop. Most small-animal vets are interested in education and will sometimes arrange a visit to the surgery or come into school to talk to the children.

In PE or dance sessions get the children to move like animals: hopping, sliding, jumping, creeping, trotting, crawling and scampering. They could listen to and then mime *Peter and the Wolf*.

RELIGIOUS EDUCATION

Read stories about St Francis of Assisi. Find out more about Buddhist attitudes to animals, and why the cow is sacred in India. Talk with the children about caring for pets, for all animals and for our whole environment.

ENVIRONMENTAL STUDIES

Discuss the lifestyles of different pets and compare these with the natural habitats of the animals. Some pets, like cats and dogs, can share our homes, but others need a special place to live which is much more like their natural habitat. Tropical fish, for example, need heat and light

and water; gerbils need soil to burrow in; guinea pigs need a well-bedded hutch, since they only feel secure and relaxed in a close environment; pet birds need an open airy aviary with room enough to fly.

PETS 6: Caring for pets

This sheet can be used to teach the children more about different pets' lifestyles and daily routines of care. You can use it to keep a record of the daily routines for school pets, each child completing it when he or she takes a turn at a particular job during one day. Each child ticks a box when his or her job is done. It can also be used by children to keep a record of their own pet's daily care, and a selection of completed records can be displayed for comparison and to illustrate the daily needs of different animals. The layout of the sheets allows for flexible use to suit a range of pets.

Protecting pets

Discuss security and cleanliness of cages and living conditions. Pets need extra protection on certain occasions, such as bonfire night; and dogs should not be let out alone as they may cause an accident to themselves or to people. All pets should be protected from pesticides and weedkillers, and litter may also be harmful to pets.

PETS 7: Find the dog!

This open-maze hand-control exercise can be used to reinforce teaching about the importance of keeping dogs under control and off the streets.

Pets and germs

Some diseases can be passed from pets to humans, so teach the children to wash their hands after handling and to avoid face contact. Pet foods, bowls and utensils should also be kept separate and washed separately to minimise the risk of infection. Toilet training of cats and dogs is vital, and gardens and footpaths should be kept clean. Dogs can also be trained in obedience to minimise the risk of accidents and increase the pleasure in owning and having the companionship of a dog.

Working animals

Some animals that we often consider only as pets actually do a job of work – jobs that humans are unable to do, e.g. police dogs and horses, gun dogs, sheep-dogs, guide dogs. Police dogs and guide dogs are the best dogs to invite into school, as they are very well trained and used to human society. Try to find out about Companion dog schemes, through which owners and their dogs visit people who are alone or in hospital.

Animals in entertainment

Not all performing animals are pets (e.g. lions), but some are (e.g. dogs, horses). Discuss whether we can tell if an animal is happy in its 'work', and whether or not it should be permitted for animals – especially large 'wild' animals – to be kept in close quarters to perform.

Pet shop

Pets 1

Give each pet its food.   Draw matching lines.

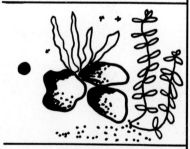

Pets 2

26

Take each pet to its bed.

Pets 3

27

Feeding pets

Our pet

Our pet is a _____ .

It is _____ old.

This is what our pet eats and drinks each day.

On Monday		
On Tuesday		
On Wednesday		
On Thursday		
On Friday		
On Saturday		
On Sunday		

Pets 4

28

Pets 5

29

Caring for pets

This is my pet _____.

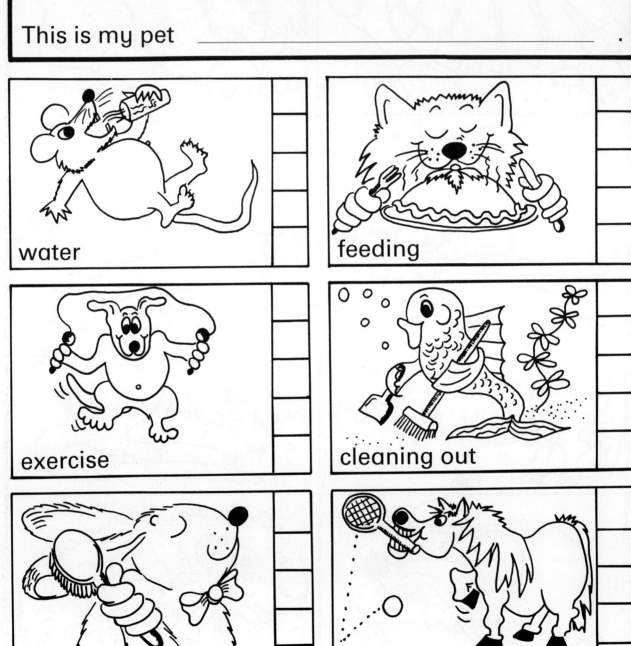

water

feeding

exercise

cleaning out

grooming

training and play

Pets 6

30

Find the dog!

Pets 7

31

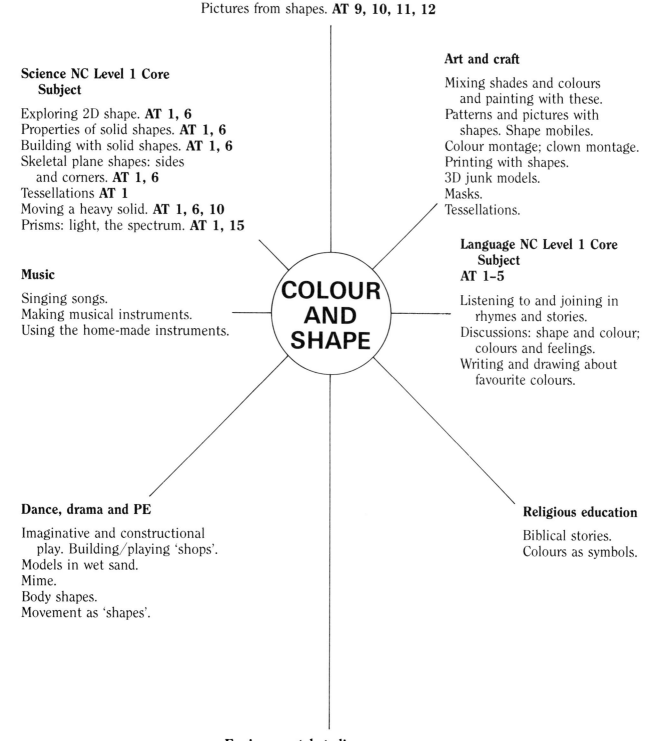

**Mathematics NC Level 1 Core
Subject**

Identifying primary colours
    and plane and solid shapes. **AT 1, 9**
Sorting, set formation, matching.
    AT 1, 2, 9, 10, 12
Shopping: different containers. **AT 1, 9, 12**
Simple tessellations. **AT 1, 9, 10, 11, 12**
Shape/colour patterns. **AT 1, 9, 10, 11, 12**
Games. **AT 9, 14**
Pictures from shapes. **AT 9, 10, 11, 12**

Art and craft

Mixing shades and colours
    and painting with these.
Patterns and pictures with
    shapes. Shape mobiles.
Colour montage; clown montage.
Printing with shapes.
3D junk models.
Masks.
Tessellations.

**Science NC Level 1 Core
Subject**

Exploring 2D shape. **AT 1, 6**
Properties of solid shapes. **AT 1, 6**
Building with solid shapes. **AT 1, 6**
Skeletal plane shapes: sides
    and corners. **AT 1, 6**
Tessellations **AT 1**
Moving a heavy solid. **AT 1, 6, 10**
Prisms: light, the spectrum. **AT 1, 15**

**Language NC Level 1 Core
Subject
AT 1–5**

Listening to and joining in
    rhymes and stories.
Discussions: shape and colour;
    colours and feelings.
Writing and drawing about
    favourite colours.

Music

Singing songs.
Making musical instruments.
Using the home-made instruments.

COLOUR AND SHAPE

Dance, drama and PE

Imaginative and constructional
    play. Building/playing 'shops'.
Models in wet sand.
Mime.
Body shapes.
Movement as 'shapes'.

Religious education

Biblical stories.
Colours as symbols.

Environmental studies

Shape and colour in the man-made
and natural environments.

COLOUR AND SHAPE

1 There are many colours. Each has a different name, and we need to learn these.

2 Some things always stay the same colour; other things change colour.

3 There are five main colours: red, blue, yellow, black and white.

4 We can mix the main colours to make other colours.

5 There are many different shapes all around us. Each has a different name, and we need to learn these.

6 We need to learn how many sides each shape has; this helps us to remember the names.

7 Some shapes are flat (plane shapes) and some are solid.

8 Some shapes fit together without leaving gaps and some do not.

9 We can build with solid shapes that fit together.

STARTING POINT

This topic is best introduced at the beginning of the autumn term and spread over that term as the teacher sees fit. A good starting point is a colour table for each of the colours, one at a time, over a period of weeks. Children can contribute to the table by bringing in their own appropriately coloured things from home. Some characters in reading schemes have 'colour' names, for example *One, Two, Three and Away* features Roger Red Hat, Billy Blue Hat, etc. If your own reading scheme is different, you can still use individual stories to introduce colour. Traditional stories and rhymes can be useful too, for example *Little Red Riding Hood, Little Boy Blue, Goldilocks and The Three Bears*. Use a popular story or cartoon character, like Postman Pat, to introduce your colour table. Draw a picture and write a caption including the colour word, then encourage the children to look for the colour in the classroom.

Read *Mr Men* stories to introduce shape. Draw pictures of characters like Mr Circle, Mr Square and Mr Triangle. Introduce plane shapes first; leave solid shapes until later in the term.

LANGUAGE

The children can listen to, discuss and learn the nursery rhymes, and join in with the stories suggested as initial stimuli. Identify and talk about the colours and shapes.

Activities for young children usually involve both language and number work, so the children should be getting a great deal of language development through mathematical work such as sorting and classifying ('These are all blue. These are all triangles.',etc.). When the children are capable of under-writing, they can draw pictures of appropriate objects and under-write simple sentences such as 'I can see a red ball', 'This is Mr Triangle'. Those with good hand-control can draw around shapes as well as drawing them free-hand.

After much discussion the children may be able to talk about their feelings related to colour, e.g. 'Red makes me feel warm.' Little written work is possible, but oral language development is very important at this stage, stimulated by observation and discussion.

COLOUR AND SHAPE 1: The clown

This shape-completion exercise practises some hand-writing movements besides helping with plane-shape recognition. The completed clown can be coloured.

COLOUR AND SHAPE 2: Identification of colours and shapes

This activity requires children to discriminate between shapes and to colour them as directed. Afterwards the children can identify the shapes in their own classroom: 'The window is square.' 'The clock is a circle.' When the children are able to attempt their own writing, they can write a few sentences about 'My favourite colour' and the things that are that colour. Their own drawings can accompany this work.

MATHEMATICS

Identify plane shapes first. Start by using coloured plastic or card shapes which the children sort for *one* property: colour *or* shape. Give the children small PE hoops for use as set rings. When they are capable, ask them to sort for *two* properties: colour *and* shape. The hoops can be overlapped to form an intersection.

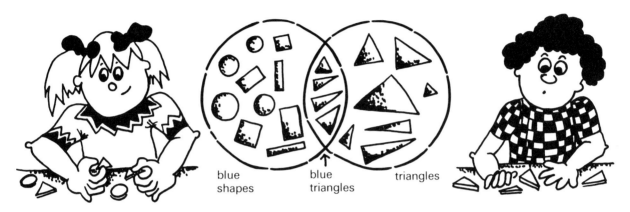

blue shapes   blue triangles   triangles

COLOUR AND SHAPE 3: Matching

In each horizontal line, the children ring the shape that matches the one in the box at the beginning of the line.

COLOUR AND SHAPE 4: Spin a shape

Make a hexagonal spinner showing the four shapes, coloured as shown, and with two blank sections.

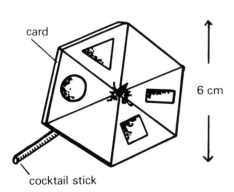

card

6 cm

cocktail stick

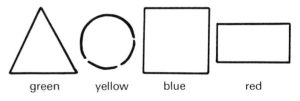

green   yellow   blue   red

This is a game for 4 players (each child picks one shape), or 2 players (each child picks two shapes). Make sure pencils of the appropriate colours are available. The children take turns to spin. If the spinner lands on a shape, the child who picked that shape can colour in one in his or her set on the photocopied sheet. If the spinner lands on a blank, the child misses a go. The winner is the first to achieve a complete coloured set.

COLOUR AND SHAPE 5: Patterns

Children complete the patterns by colouring the shapes. Let the children give the creatures names.

Solid shapes

Turn the home corner into a shop and ask the children to bring in lots of boxes and containers of different shapes.

Make large labels: These are cuboids (cylinders, spheres, cubes), and give the children large hoops so that they can sort the containers into sets. You could paint some of the containers so that the sorting can be for shape and colour.

SCIENCE

All the activities should be practical and involve much discussion. Sort solid shapes for locomotive and tessellating properties, and relate any findings to the use of shapes in the world outside school, e.g. wheels are 'round' (like very shallow cylinders) and they move smoothly; walls are made up of shapes that fit together firmly without leaving gaps. You will need a smooth surface inclined at an angle of about 45° to test the shapes for sliding and rolling.

COLOUR AND SHAPE 6: Properties of solid shapes

This sheet can be used to record what the children find out from the experiments already mentioned, and from stacking and building activities. Try building walls and towers – and even castles – with the various shapes. Encourage the children to discuss what they have done, and write short sentences to accompany drawings:

I can build with these shapes.
I can put these shapes on top of one another.
These shapes fit together well.
These shapes do not fit together well.

Investigations

Briefly, here are some other investigations you might try.

Let the children construct skeletal plane shapes using plastic Meccano® or Constructastraws® (or plastic drink-ing straws and pipe-cleaners). Try triangles, squares, rectangles, pentagons and hexagons. The children should count the sides and corners.

Present the children with this problem: how can they move a large wooden storage crate containing two children across the hall or playground? There should be rollers available so that eventually – maybe with your help – the children will discover that movement is much easier when rollers are moved from the back to the front of the crate as it is moved across the ground. Let the children try pushing without rollers, then pulling, then pushing with rollers, then pulling. Which technique works worst? best?

Use prisms to find out more about the spectrum, light and the colours of the rainbow, at a level appropriate for the children.

ART AND CRAFT

Mixing colours and painting

Mix white with a primary colour, a little at a time. On a large sheet of paper paint a strip of the pure primary colour, then paint successive strips each time a bit more white is added.

Mix two colours to produce a third: blue and yellow for green; red and blue for purple; red and white for pink; red and yellow for orange; and so on. Let the children paint freely with these 'made' colours.

Paint on wet paper so that the children can observe how the colours change as the paints mix together.

Shape patterns and colour montage

Cut out lots of different shapes from gummed paper. The children can try to do this, but usually they will find following the cutting lines too difficult. Suggest that the children each create a pattern using a single shape, say circles of all different sizes, or different triangles. These can be mounted on cards of the same shape as the pattern pieces, and hung from the ceiling or on the wall, with appropriate labels.

Using more of the same gummed shapes, but the whole range this time, the children can create pictures. Stylised figures, trains, buildings and boats are fairly easy starters.

For the montage, collect lots of different shades of, say, blue, from magazines and catalogues. Make a blue montage. You could make a montage 'rainbow'.

Collage figure

This activity combines work on colour, texture and shape because the figure is made of different fabric shapes. Here is one possible design.

Shape printing

Collect tubes, boxes, cartons and containers of as many different shapes as possible, particularly those with unusual cross-sections (e.g. Toblerone® boxes). Dip the ends, or sides, in thick paint and make shape prints. You could produce Plasticine® shapes of your own and print with those.

Junk models

Make models from junk solid shapes; they can be abstract or representational. Talk about the difficulties of gluing curved surfaces, awkward joints, etc. If appropriate, link the activity with your CDT work.

Masks

Paper plates are ideal as basic masks. They can be decorated in all sorts of ways to produce faces, flowers, suns, etc.

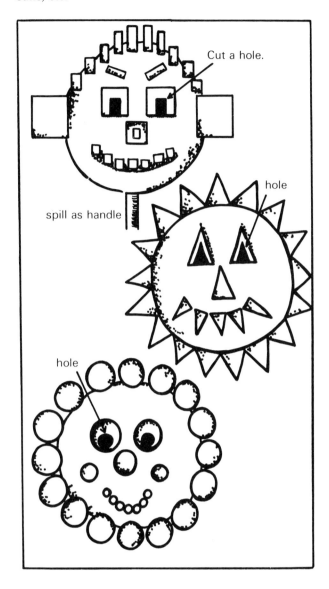

Tessellations

Use gummed-paper shapes to explore the properties of tessellating shapes. The shapes can be stuck on to a backing sheet so that you have a record of shapes which fit together without leaving any spaces and shapes which leave spaces.

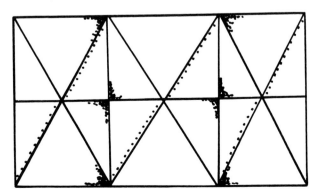

MUSIC

Sing songs that mention colours: 'I can Sing a Rainbow'; 'Lavender's Blue'; 'I have seen the Golden Sunshine'; 'Every Colour under the Sun' (from the book of the same name, published by Ward Lock Educational).

Make musical instruments from some of the solid shapes you have collected, and use them to accompany your singing.

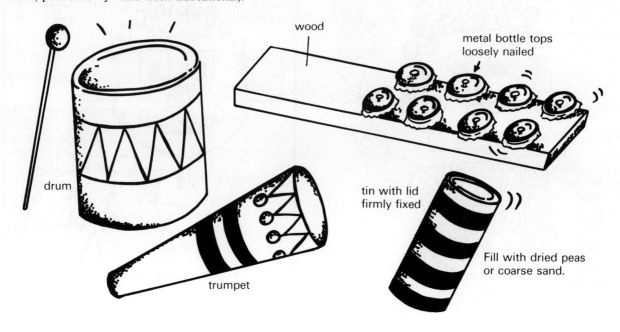

DANCE, DRAMA AND PE

Imaginative and constructional play

Use large cardboard boxes and outdoor playblocks to make castles, boats, trains, houses, caves, and so on.

Play 'shops' with the containers collected for the mathematical activities.

Use wet sand and various containers to make 3D models: castles, trains, flats, etc.

Drama

Read or improvise stories about colours and then let groups of children mime them.

Movement

Working singly or in pairs, the children can make various shapes with their own bodies: sphere (curl up in a ball); triangle (make an 'angle' and use the floor as the third side). Small groups could make interlocking shapes.

Ask the children to move around the hall in the manner of 3D shapes: rolling (sphere, cylinder); rolling in a curve (cone); sliding (cube and cuboid).

RELIGIOUS EDUCATION

Tell the stories of Noah and the rainbow and Joseph and his coat of many colours. Find out about colours as symbols, e.g. for Christians, white is a symbol of purity; for the Chinese, red is a very lucky colour.

38

ENVIRONMENTAL STUDIES

Look for colours in school and the local environment. Look for shapes as well: windows, doors, roofs, fences, church spires, towers, manhole covers, toys in the park. Notice how bricks and paving stones tessellate. Make a large class frieze of all you saw on a walk around school.

COLOUR AND SHAPE 7: I-spy

Children look for shapes in the picture to correspond with those shown at the foot of the sheet. Once a child finds, say, a triangle, he or she colours it in the picture and ticks the triangle at the foot. Then the child should try to spot that shape in the classroom.

Take the children for a neighbourhood walk. Look for natural shapes and colours, preferably in specific contexts, e.g. colours for camouflage, as warnings, in seasonal changes, on young animals in comparison to adults, rainbows, new leaves; spiral shells, spiders' webs, crystals, frogspawn. Natural tessellations are difficult to actually find, but talk about honeycomb and pineapple skin.

Complete the shapes.   Then colour the clown.

Colour and shape 1

40

Colour the circles red.
Colour the squares orange.

circle

square

Colour and shape 2

41

In each row, match the shape in the box.
Draw a line round the one which is the same.

Colour and shape 3

Spin a shape

green

red

yellow

blue

Colour and shape 4

43

Complete the patterns by colouring the shapes.

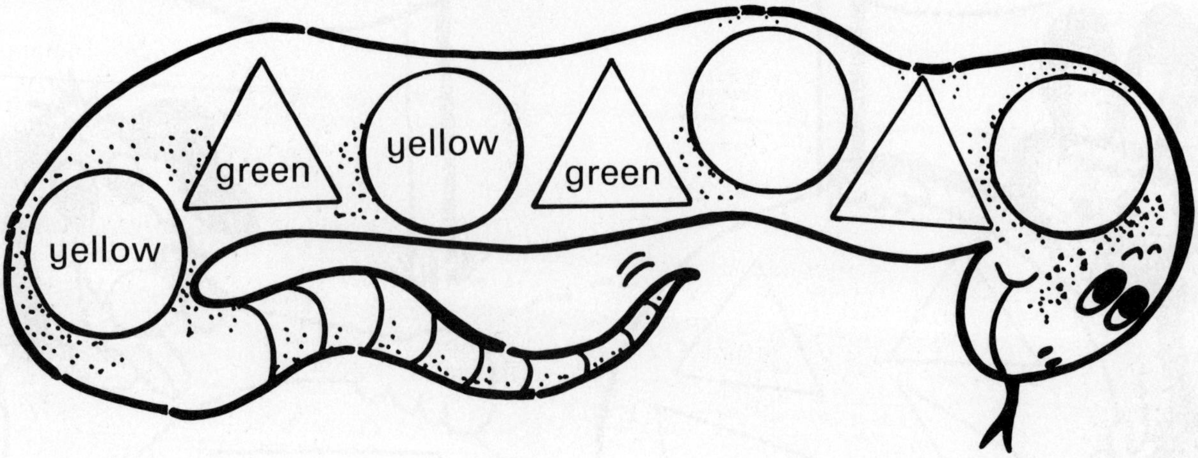

yellow green yellow green

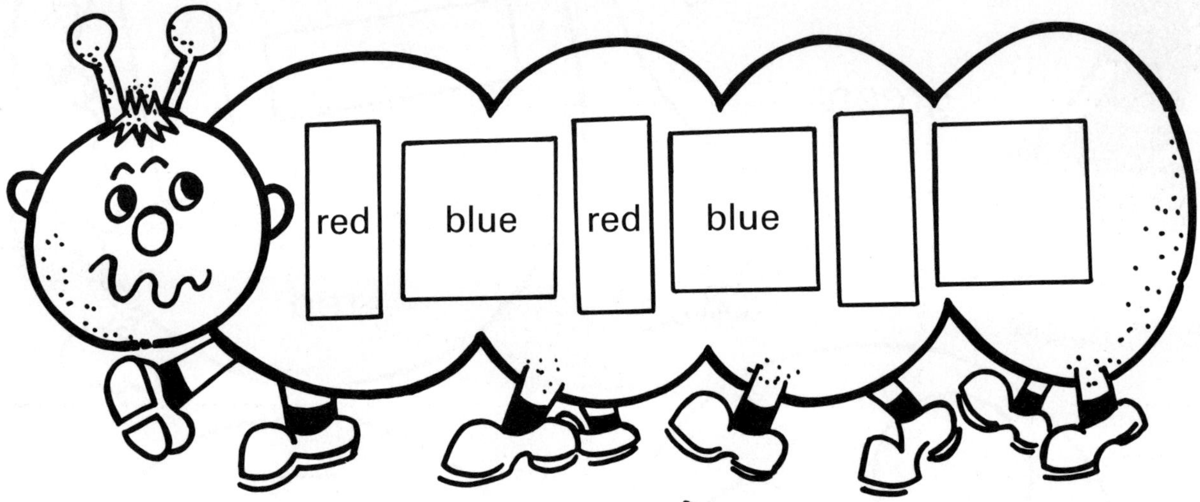

red blue red blue

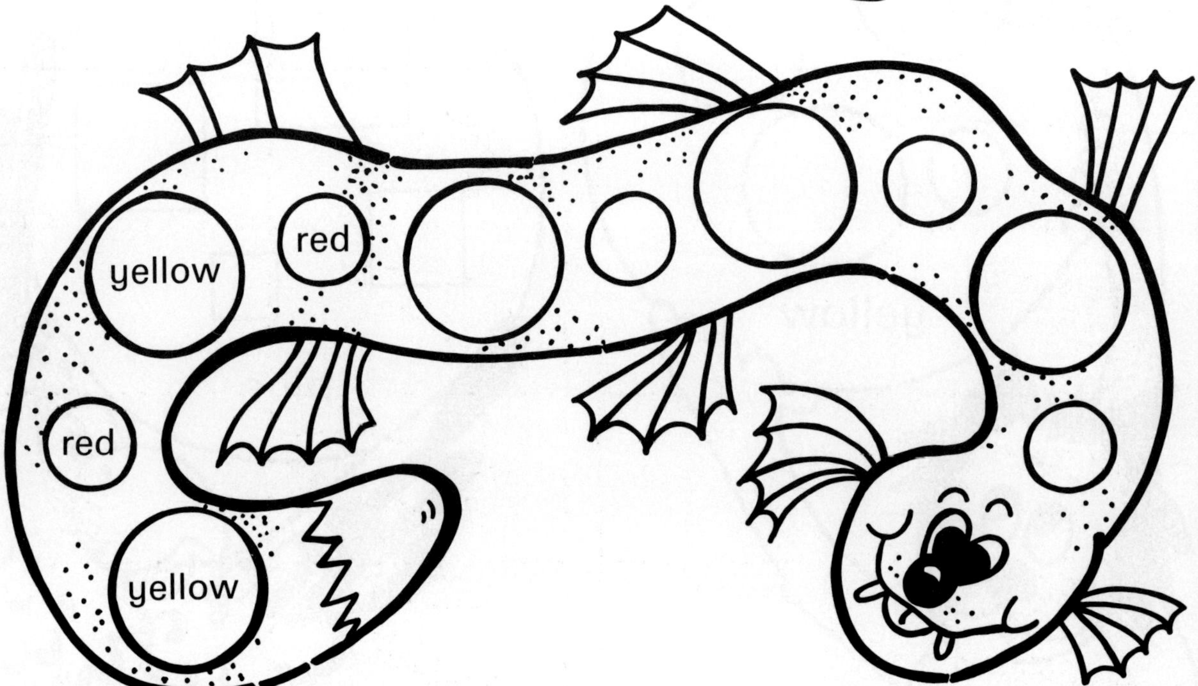

yellow red

red

yellow

Colour and shape 5

44

What can you do with shapes?

Try rolling and sliding.

These shapes roll.	Tick for yes

These shapes slide.	Tick for yes

Colour and shape 6

45

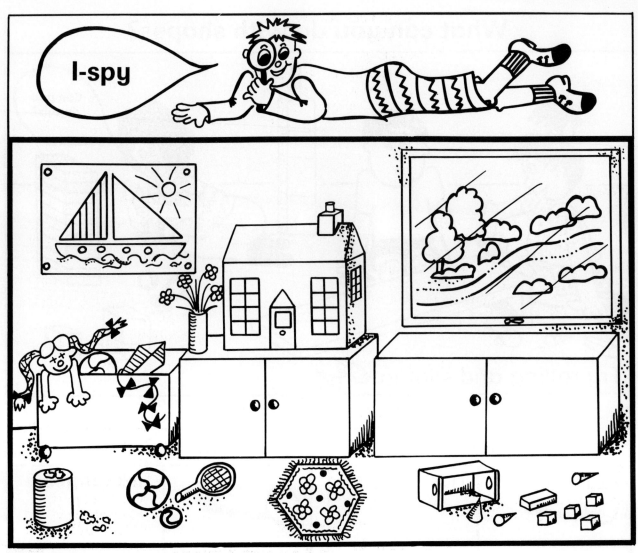

I-spy

Find each shape in the picture.
Tick the shape here. Colour the shape in the picture.

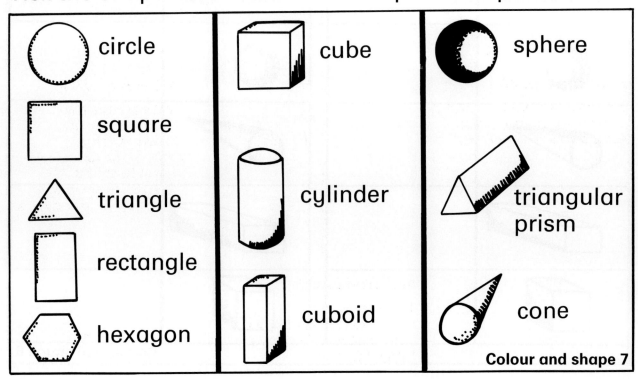

circle

square

triangle

rectangle

hexagon

cube

cylinder

cuboid

sphere

triangular prism

cone

Colour and shape 7

46

Mathematics NC Level 2 Core Subject

Simple games: number recognition; counting on and back in ones. **AT 1, 9, 14**
Comparison: capacity of containers. **AT 1, 8, 9**

Science NC Level 2 Core Subject

Experiments exploring water as a solid, a liquid and a gas: floating and sinking; ice expands; refraction; surface tension; air and water pressure; water power; convection currents; dissolving and diluting; chromatography; evaporation and condensation. The water cycle. **AT 1, 2, 6, 9, 10, 13, 15**

Art and craft

Mixing paint.
Painting growth patterns in tones of colour.
Blob and blow patterns.
Reflections.
Bubble prints. String patterns.
Marbling.
Wax-resist.
Tie-and-dye.

Music

Listening to music.
Singing.
Composing sound pictures.
Improvising water sounds.

WATER

Language NC Level 2 Core Subject AT 1–5

Listening to and reading poems and stories.
Reportive writing: visits, activities, experiments.
Imaginative writing.

Dance, drama and PE

Improvised movements to suggest the various states of water.
Mimed stories and characters.

Religious education

Water as a life-source.
Aid in times of flood and drought.
Biblical stories.
Christian baptism.
Water in other religious ceremonies and festivals.

Environmental studies

The water cycle.
Uses of water: past and present.
Water hobbies and activities.
Safety. Pollution.

WATER

BASIC CONCEPTS

1 Every living thing needs water.

2 More than half the world is covered by water.

3 Water moves from land to air and back to the land in a constant cycle: the water cycle.

4 Water can be a solid, a liquid or a gas.

5 Water can be useful: for example, for warmth, cleaning and energy.

6 Water can be dangerous.

7 Water can be fun.

8 Water can be beautiful.

STARTING POINT

Collect lots of pictures of different areas of water, such as lakes, rivers, seas and canals. Try to obtain pictures depicting the different moods of water: tranquil pools, crashing waves, waterfalls, water as sources of power (millstream and hydro-electric power station).

If possible visit an area of water nearby: go on a boat trip or a canal walk. Try to visit a harbour or dockyard, or a maritime museum where you can usually see many different types of craft for use in commerce or for pleasure. Ask the children if they or their relatives engage in any water sports and, if possible, borrow some equipment to make a class display of armbands, life-jackets, inflatable balls, a lilo, snorkel, flippers, etc.

Stories to read could include *The Little Mermaid*, *Tidalick*, and *Wet Albert*. Read poems and sing songs about anything concerned with water: the sea, rainbows, clouds, storms, fog, snow, ice, and so on. Natural history videos include extracts about water; if the commentary is too advanced, turn down the sound and let the children ask their own questions.

LANGUAGE

WATER 1: Water is . . .

This sheet shows many different aspects of water and can be used as a cover for a topic book or as a general writing page.

WATER 2: Life in water

There are two pages in one on this sheet; marine and freshwater life. Block off the unwanted half with a sheet of paper before photocopying. This sheet can be used to report on a pond-dipping excursion, a visit to a marine aquarium, a fish market, watching video material, or to contrast the two environments. If pollution is a current topic, the children could use the blank part of each sheet to draw the pollutants which threaten each environment.

The blank areas can also be used for imaginative writing about deep-sea diving or life as one of the creatures pictured.

WATER 3: Games

Silly sea-monsters: Make a spinner with black and white segments, which the children use in turn. If the spinner lands on black the child can draw a foot on his or her monster. If it lands on white the child misses that turn. The winner is the first to achieve a monster with 6 completed feet. *Fishy fun-time:* The same rules apply as for the previous game, but the children draw the fish-scales instead of feet. For more able children use standard dice, with rules such as only being able to draw a foot or scale when a 2, 4 or 6 is thrown.

WATER 4: Race round the rocks

This game is played on an unnumbered line. The children take turns to throw a dice and move a counter according to the dice number thrown. There are simple forfeits and gains involving the child in a move back one place or forward one place, but they are not, at this stage, asked to move on or back on a number line. You may need an adult or older child to help to read the forfeits and gains.

Capacity

Collect a range of containers which hold roughly the same amount but which are different in shape. Ask the children to experiment in order to find out which holds the most, or the least. You will need a large water trough, a jug and a range of containers.

SCIENCE

WATER 5: Floating and sinking

This is a simple chart for classifying 'floaters' and 'sinkers'. You will need a selection of objects for the children to test (some are shown on the sheet) and a small transparent plastic tank of water. Let the children do the testing themselves, but discuss possibilities beforehand and encourage predictions. Ask questions: 'Do some things float beneath the surface?' 'What do you think makes things float?' 'Can we refloat things that have sunk?' To demonstrate the latter, blow air into a submerged bottle. Also, a lump of Plasticine® will sink, but if you shape it like a boat and place it on the water with care it will float.

Water can be a solid, a liquid or a gas as demonstrated by the following experiments. Encourage careful observation, questions and, where appropriate, recording. The experiments are presented in three sections, showing some of the properties of ice, water and steam or water vapour.

Ice

The children can look for ice and icicles on a very cold day. Look, too, at the shapes the ice has made; a heavy frost sometimes produces good crystal formations. Try to freeze a bubble: blow a bubble, catch it on the wire ring and place it in the freezer. With careful handling, it may be possible to observe ice crystals on the surface.

Ice needs space
Put an ice-cube into a plastic cup almost full of water. Ask the children what they think will happen when the ice-cube melts; then wait and see. In fact, the level of the water will stay about the same because the water in the ice takes up less space than the ice itself.

Fill a bottle with water and make a loose-fitting top out of tinfoil. Put the bottle in the freezer. When the water has frozen, you will find that the top has been pushed up by the expanding ice. (The children can do this experiment at home.)

Water as a liquid

Refraction

A straw will appear bent when placed in water in a shallow clear-plastic dish and viewed from the side.

Put a coin in the bottom of a plastic tub and, looking down on the tub, move your head until you cannot see the coin. Pour in water and the edge of the coin will appear. Take care not to move your head.

Surface tension

Use an eye-dropper to fill a narrow container to the very top. From a side view you should be able to see the curved surface of the water.

Tie one end of a piece of string to the handle of a jug, pass it over the lip of the jug and hold the other end firmly in position on the far side of an empty container. Hold jug and container apart so that the string is pulled tight and, holding the jug over the container, pour the water from the jug down the string. Once the flow has started, lower the jug so that it is at an angle – the water should continue to flow down the string.

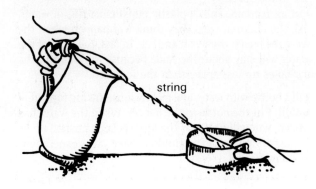

string

Make five holes the same size, and evenly spaced, at the bottom of a container. Hold the container under a tap and five separate streams of water will emerge. However, if you 'pinch' the streams together, they will cling to each other, forming one stream united by surface tension.

Bubbles are a result of surface tension. To make bubble mixture, put 3 to 4 tablespoons of soap powder or soap flakes into 4 cupfuls of hot water. Stir in the soap and leave the mixture to stand for three days. Then add a large spoonful of sugar. To make a blower, bend a piece of wire into a circle (or any other continuous shape). Try 3D shapes: a cube, pyramid or spiral. Look carefully at the film made by the soapy water.

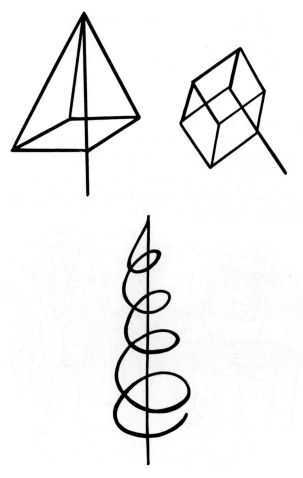

Despite its holes, a small plastic 'strawberry basket' will float on the surface of a bowl of water, if placed there carefully. However, if you drop a tissue into the basket, the surface tension will be broken and the basket will sink.

Air pressure and water

Hold a glass at an angle and slide it, rim first, under the surface of the water. Bubbles of air will escape until the rim is completely submerged. Hold the glass upright and lift it slightly, but do not let the rim rise above the surface. The level of the water inside the glass will be higher than that in the bowl, because air pressure on the surface of the water in the bowl prevents the water level in the glass falling. Lift the rim of the glass above the surface and air is allowed in the glass. This air will push the water down to the same level as that in the bowl.

Warm water rises

To make an underwater 'volcano', fill a small glass bottle with hot water and add one or two drops of ink or food colouring. Tie string around the neck.

Fill a large glass or plastic jar with cold water and carefully lower the small bottle into it. The coloured hot water will rise up through the cold water.

Water power

To make a simple water-wheel, cut the bottom from an aluminium foil pie-dish and then make cuts from the edge towards the centre, as shown. Twist each section carefully until it is at right angles to the centre. Push a pencil through the centre and hold each end gently with finger and thumb. Now hold the wheel under a slow-running tap and, as the water strikes the blades, the wheel will turn.

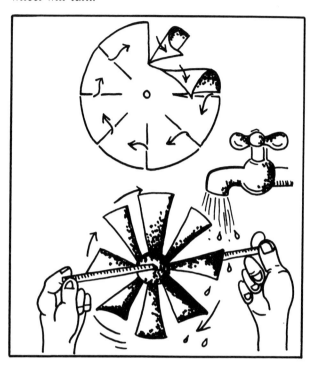

Water power through pressure

Fill plastic squeezy bottles with water and experiment to discover the effects of gentle, strong and very strong 'squeezes' on the speed at which the water shoots out of the top and how far it travels. Hold a competition to see who can shoot water furthest (go outside first!).

To make a 'water tower', punch 3 small holes of equal size up the side of a squeezy bottle. Cover the holes with tape and then fill the bottle with water. Remove the tape to see which hole lets out the longest jet of water. The bottom hole will do this because the water at the bottom of the bottle is under the greatest pressure.

Dissolving things in water

Collect different substances such as sugar, soap powder, tea-leaves, coffee powder, sand and sawdust. Using a separate container for each substance, see what happens when a teaspoonful of each is placed at the bottom and you pour on cold water, warm water, hot water, stir the mixture, do not stir the mixture. Only those substances that go into solution can be said to dissolve in the water, e.g. sugar. Sand does not dissolve; it disperses when stirred, but soon settles back on the bottom.

WATER 6: Water can dissolve things

This sheet provides a means of recording the results of the experiments about dissolving. These experiments are, perhaps, best conducted as a group or class activity. In any case, adult supervision is essential when hot water is involved. Use the sheet for children's individual records of their observations, and to give practice in forming conclusions. Note that there is room on the sheet for recording results with four more substances of your choice.

Dilution

Make orange squash by adding the concentrated orange a bit at a time, to find the best mix. Record as you go along. Try different brands and use controlled amounts of water. When something is diluted it is made less concentrated usually by adding water or a thinner.

Chromatography

You will need filter paper, a tube of Smarties® and/or a black water-based felt-tip pen. Sort out single Smarties® of different colours and place each on its own disk of filter paper on a saucer. Drop a few drops of water onto each, and watch what happens. To use the pen, draw a dot on a circle of filter paper and drop the water on that.

Some of the colour deposits can be quite unexpected, which makes the patterns more interesting.

Steam

Note that the experiments in this section must be done **by the teacher**, as must all activities involving hot water.

Disappearing water

Fill a small pan with water to a depth of 1 cm. Boil off the water until the pan is empty. Watch the steam rise. Discuss where the water has gone (into the air as water vapour).

Steam is water

Cut the bottom off a large clear-plastic lemonade bottle (leave the top on) to make a bell jar. Fill a small container with boiling water and place the bell jar over it. The steam will rapidly fill the jar and will eventually condense into water droplets on the side of the jar.

The colour in each Smartie® and in the pen is actually produced by a mixture of a lot of different colours. These dissolve at different rates and so, as they percolate through the filter paper, they form patterns. The colours nearest the centre are those which dissolve quickest.

Note: Under the heading 'Environmental studies', please see the notes on photocopiable sheet 7: the water cycle. You may prefer to use the sheet at this point.

Painting

Mix water-based paints with black or white to produce different tones. The children can paint 'growth' patterns using various shades of the same colour. For example, they could paint concentric rings like tree rings, or banded fan-shapes, or ripples produced in a pond by a pebble. A growth pattern is simply a pattern that grows – it need not represent anything. Start with a dot in one corner and take the first line from the dot to anywhere on the page and back to the dot. The next line follows the one before, and so on until the paper is completely covered.

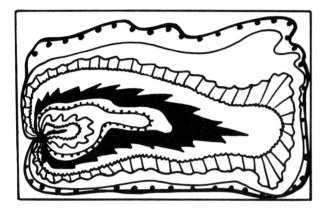

Drop blobs of fairly wet paint onto wet paper. The colours will spread and merge to create interesting patterns.

Paint a waterscape on the top half of a piece of paper (fold the paper prior to painting). Paint down to the fold, and make sure the paint is wet in all areas; then fold to print the 'reflection'.

Prints and patterns

To make bubble prints, mix water-based paints with washing-up liquid and put each colour into a separate plastic tub. Use a straw to blow a good head of bubbles on a tub and 'print' this by placing a piece of paper over the tub. Do this several times, with similar or contrasting colours, to create patterns.

To make string patterns, dip lengths of absorbent string into pots of paint, leaving both ends of each piece dry. Once a piece of string is well soaked, place it in a wavy pattern on a sheet of paper. Place another sheet of paper on top, making sure that both ends are sticking out, and then put a board on top of the two sheets. While a partner presses down on the board, pull the string out by both ends. Lift the board and top sheet. What patterns appear on the sheets?

The 'blob and blow' technique involves dropping a blob of watery paint onto paper and blowing it around through a straw. The blown paint leaves spidery tracks. Add more blobs of different coloured paints and blow them around to make interesting patterns. For particularly effective results use black or white paint on a range of coloured papers.

Marbling

For this you will need an old washing-up bowl half full of water and a selection of oil-based paints. Using a brush, drop paint onto the water; you can use several colours or just two, and swirl the pattern with the brush if you wish. Your paper should be no bigger than the bowl. Simply lay it on the surface and lift it out by one edge. Handle it carefully, shake off excess water and dry flat.

Wax-resist

Draw a picture or pattern on cartridge paper, using wax crayon applied thickly. Then colour wash all over the sheet with a contrasting water-based paint. The waxed areas will resist the water and only the unwaxed paper will colour.

Tie-and-dye

Tie a piece of white or light-coloured cotton material, using string or elastic bands. The ties, which must be tight, can be in different places, as shown. Soak the tied cloth in a cold-water dye, then unknot and dry it. Iron the cloth before mounting.

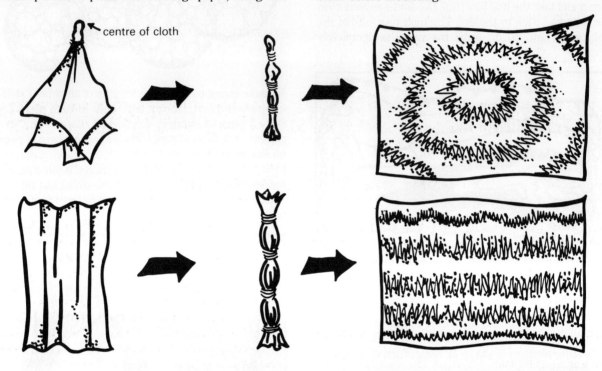

MUSIC

Listen to pieces of music inspired by water-related subjects: *Raindrop Prelude* by Beethoven; the *Trout* piano quintet by Schubert; *Fingal's Cave* by Mendelssohn; and *Swan Lake* by Tchaikovsky.

Sing songs like 'I Can Sing a Rainbow'; 'Oh I Do Like to Be Beside the Seaside'; 'Raindrops Keep Falling on my Head'; and 'Singing in the Rain'.

Use non-tuned percussion instruments to make watery sounds, e.g. a run on a glockenspiel could represent a rainbow to the children, maracas may sound like raindrops and cymbals like a splash. You can also use junk material to make sounds to accompany your songs: scrunched-up Cellophane® for splashes, wooden beads rattled in a tray for bubbles popping, corrugated card used like a washboard for running water.

Make a sound-picture of a thirsty day and use it as a musical score for future performances.

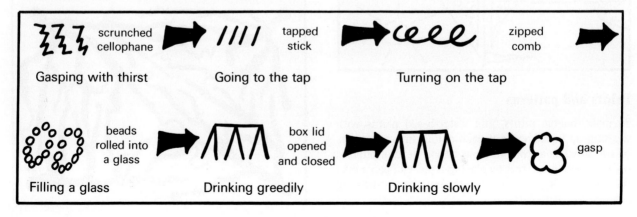

54

DANCE, DRAMA AND PE

In movement sessions improvise the states and actions of water: twirling like snow falling; spinning like water going down a plughole; stretching and jumping to represent bubbles growing and bursting; rolling for slowly flowing water; light swirling movements for steam; angular, balanced body shapes for ice formations.

The children could also mime the actions of various characters: the little mermaid, a shark, a flying fish, a heavily-weighted deep-sea diver, a sea-snake, a frog.

RELIGIOUS EDUCATION

Talk about water as a major life-source and about the need to help peoples who are suffering because of drought or floods. Tell some of the biblical stories like Noah's Ark or Jonah and the Whale. Talk about baptism and the baptismal rites in different religions – you could act out a Christian baptism or any other religious ceremony in which water plays a significant part.

ENVIRONMENTAL STUDIES

WATER 7: The water cycle

Explain the water cycle to the children, in simple terms, using the experiments about condensation to illustrate the cycle on a small scale. Let the children colour the scene on the sheet and then complete the elementary language exercise.

Using illustrated reference books, find out about and discuss how water was used in the past, industrially, domestically, for energy and for pleasure. Visit local museums for information about canals or water mills that might have functioned in your area.

Visit also any nearby river, lake, reservoir or canal to see some of the ways in which water is used today. You might even be able to take a boat trip, and there is sure to be an ice-rink and/or swimming pool reasonably close by.

Walk round the school and note where and for what water is used: e.g. for washing, for science, for the school pet, for cleaning, for school lunch. Then make a frieze to show, in order, the rooms visited, and add colourful labels to show exactly how the water is used. The children can carry out a similar survey of their own homes.

Explore water hobbies, displaying the children's own equipment and using their spoken accounts of skiing, water-skiing, diving, skating, swimming, fishing, sailing, boating, etc.

Try to identify pollutants of water. Make a large wall picture to illustrate the ways in which water can be polluted by litter, farm pesticides and fertilisers, sewage, chemicals, etc. Stress the need to conserve water and water habitats. Using video material of news items, talk about floods and droughts.

Water 1

Fresh water

Salt water

Water 2

57

Silly sea-monsters

Name

Name

Fishy fun-time

Name

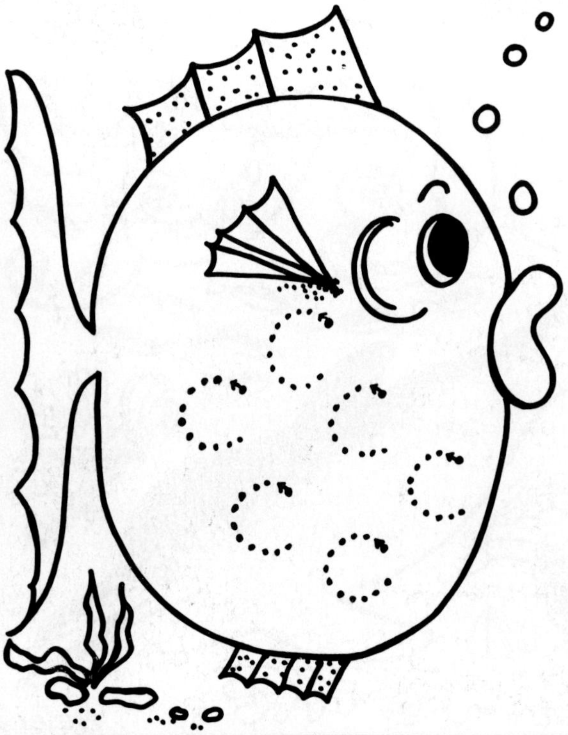

Name

Water 3

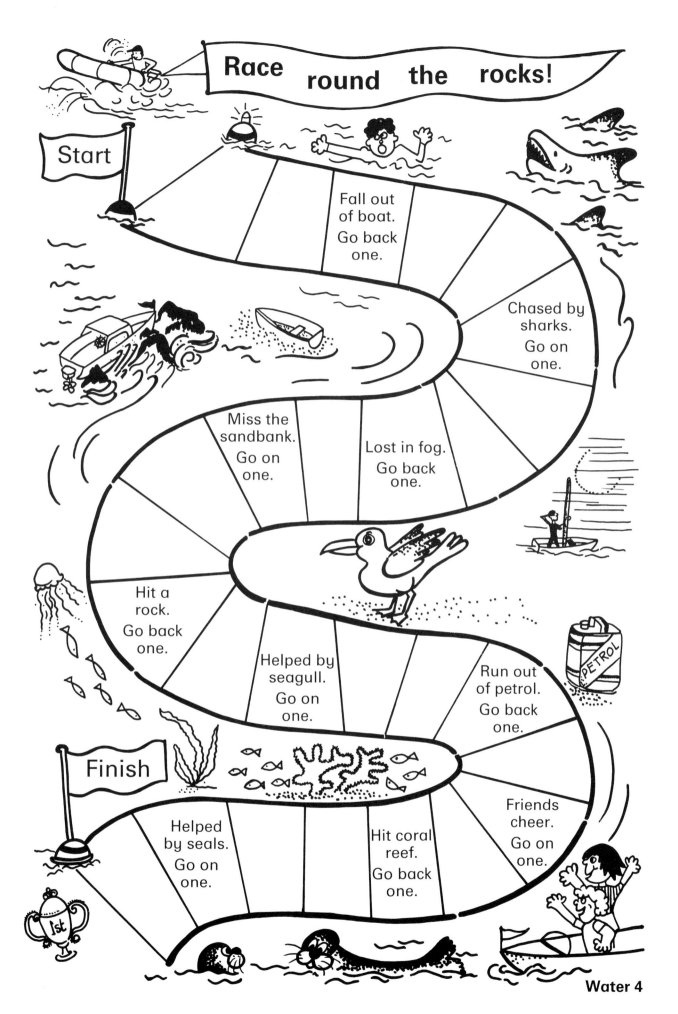

Race round the rocks!

Start

Fall out of boat. Go back one.

Chased by sharks. Go on one.

Miss the sandbank. Go on one.

Lost in fog. Go back one.

Hit a rock. Go back one.

Helped by seagull. Go on one.

Run out of petrol. Go back one.

Finish

Helped by seals. Go on one.

Hit coral reef. Go back one.

Friends cheer. Go on one.

Water 4

59

Floating and sinking

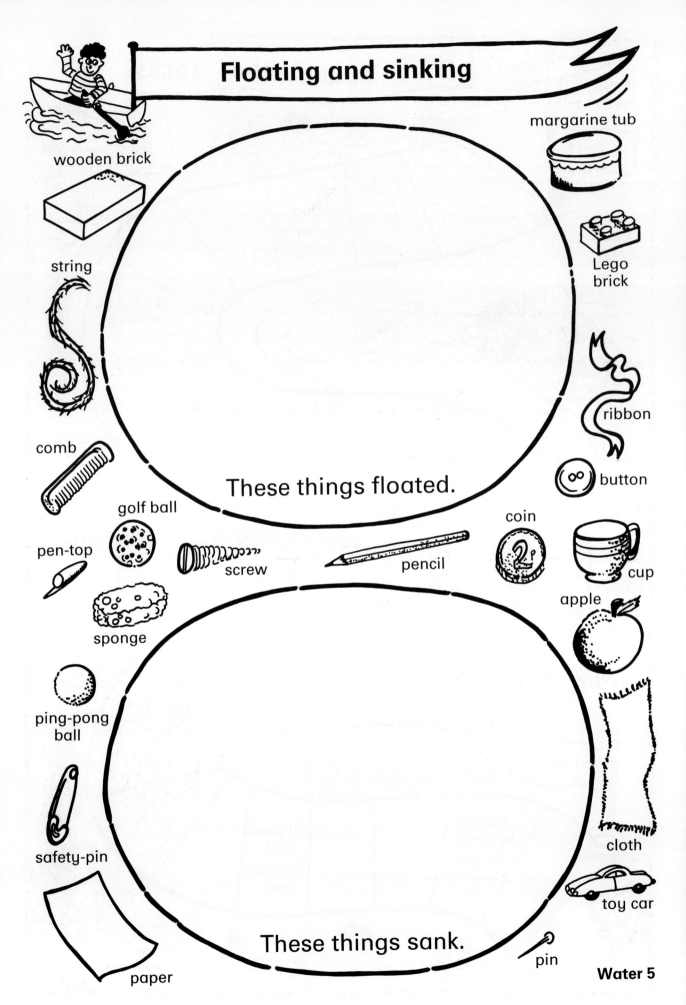

wooden brick

margarine tub

string

Lego brick

comb

ribbon

button

These things floated.

golf ball

coin

pen-top

screw

pencil

cup

sponge

apple

ping-pong ball

safety-pin

cloth

toy car

These things sank.

paper

pin

Water can dissolve things.
Tick the box if the substance dissolves:

	in cold water	in warm water	in hot water	if stirred	if not stirred
sugar					
tea leaves					
coffee					
sawdust					
soap powder					
sand					

What I found out

The water cycle

sky

cloud

rain

sun

evaporation

mountain

stream

sea

river

land

How many words begin with r ?

How many words begin with s ?

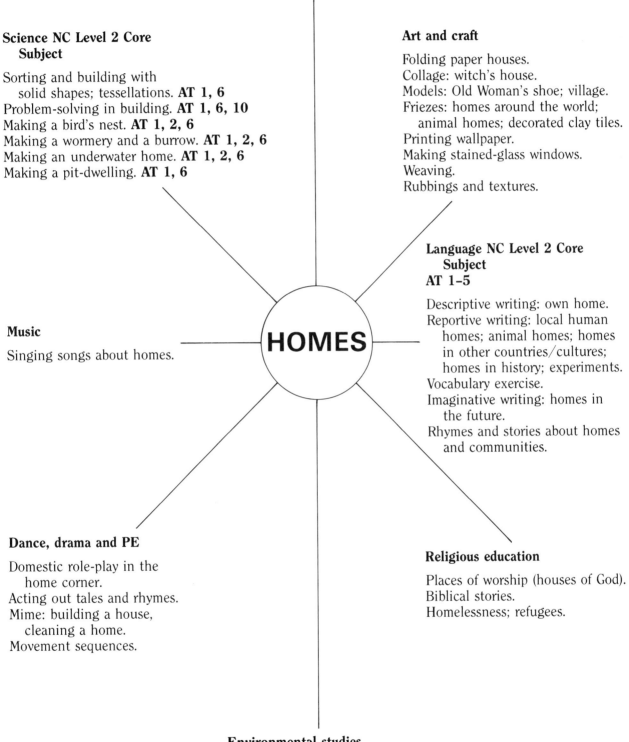

Mathematics NC Level 2 Core Subject

Identifying plane and solid shapes. **AT 1, 9, 10, 11**
Shapes in buildings. **AT 1, 9, 10, 11**
Matching activity. **AT 1, 9, 13**
Comparisons (size and shape). **AT 1, 8, 9**
Pictogram. **AT 1, 9, 12, 13**

Science NC Level 2 Core Subject

Sorting and building with
    solid shapes; tessellations. **AT 1, 6**
Problem-solving in building. **AT 1, 6, 10**
Making a bird's nest. **AT 1, 2, 6**
Making a wormery and a burrow. **AT 1, 2, 6**
Making an underwater home. **AT 1, 2, 6**
Making a pit-dwelling. **AT 1, 6**

Art and craft

Folding paper houses.
Collage: witch's house.
Models: Old Woman's shoe; village.
Friezes: homes around the world;
    animal homes; decorated clay tiles.
Printing wallpaper.
Making stained-glass windows.
Weaving.
Rubbings and textures.

Music

Singing songs about homes.

HOMES

Language NC Level 2 Core Subject AT 1–5

Descriptive writing: own home.
Reportive writing: local human
    homes; animal homes; homes
    in other countries/cultures;
    homes in history; experiments.
Vocabulary exercise.
Imaginative writing: homes in
    the future.
Rhymes and stories about homes
    and communities.

Dance, drama and PE

Domestic role-play in the
    home corner.
Acting out tales and rhymes.
Mime: building a house,
    cleaning a home.
Movement sequences.

Religious education

Places of worship (houses of God).
Biblical stories.
Homelessness; refugees.

Environmental studies

Human and animal habitats at
    home and around the world.
Homes in the past.
Communities.

63

HOMES

1 All living things need a shelter or a safe resting place.

2 Homes can be anywhere. They can be off the ground, on the ground, under the ground, on water, or underwater.

3 Both humans and animals build homes from many kinds of materials.

4 Some homes are permanent, some are temporary, and some are carried around.

STARTING POINT

Human homes

Collect pictures of all the different types of dwelling: caravan, cave, bungalow, terraced house, houseboat, mansion, etc. As a focal point for a display you could make a simple pictorial street plan of the area and the children could stick photos of their own homes in the correct places on the map.

If possible, visit a large country house. Try to contrast the lifestyles of the owners and the servants of past generations and of today.

Read stories of community and village life, e.g. *Postman Pat, Camberwick Green, Trumpton, Fireman Sam, The Wombles* and *Hansel and Gretel*. Nursery rhymes could include 'There was an Old Woman who lived in a Shoe'.

Animal homes

Collect pictures of wildlife habitats. Try to make a video compilation of information about different animal homes from wildlife programmes, e.g. the forest, the sea, tree-tops, rivers and streams, polar and tropical regions. Read animal stories, and folk-tales about characters such as Brer Rabbit and Anancy, and watch excerpts from the cartoon version of *Watership Down*.

LANGUAGE

The children could write descriptively about their own homes and what particularly they like about them, e.g. *My favourite room; My bedroom.*

HOMES 1: Human homes and animal homes

This sheet can be used as the cover for a topic booklet; or photocopied with a paper mask over first one half and then the other, to produce two sheets with space for children's written work.

Human homes

Use books and pictures to investigate and discuss homes in different countries and from different cultures. Help the children to develop research skills: looking in books for information; studying pictures for facts and details; reading labels correctly, etc. Even if the children cannot read, they can be encouraged to look at illustrated book covers and select books that are likely to be about homes.

Walk around your local area, looking at various buildings. Compare old and new. Follow this up by asking the children to write about the homes they noticed, e.g. bungalows, terraced houses, flats, farms; and any unusual homes, e.g. houseboats, caravans, barns, windmills.

On a separate occasion, discuss homes in the past. Keep the distinctions obvious – caves, castles, town houses through the ages. If you visit a stately home, let the children write about their observations and feelings.

Animal homes

Find out about the sites of animal homes, e.g. in trees, on the ground, underground, in water, on water. Using books, the children can draw and paint animals and write about them and their lifestyles.

Imaginative writing

There is plenty of scope for this: magical, strange or unusual homes, e.g. *The upside-down house; The house of the future; Space house; The moving home; The haunted house; My tree-house; Life in a toadstool.*

HOMES 2: About the house

This picture of a story-book house is designed to identify various features of a house and enlarge the children's vocabulary. Photocopy the sheet to A3 size for use as a class vocabulary display chart, and give each child an A4 copy to colour and keep in his or her topic folder for reference.

MATHEMATICS

Look around the classroom for plane and solid shapes. Then go for a walk and look for these shapes in buildings, especially homes. Compare the sizes of different homes and extend the children's vocabulary by using and talking about terms like *shorter, longer, bigger, smaller, high, low, wide, narrow.*

HOMES 3: Homes and shapes

This is a simple matching exercise to draw children's attention to shapes in buildings. Talk with the children about the homes and shapes. The church is the 'house' of God.

Make a pictogram of the homes in which children live: detached, semi-detached, terraced, flats, farms, bungalows, etc. Use the children's own drawings or paintings (make sure they all use paper of the same size).

SCIENCE

Building

Collect as many cardboard boxes as you can, of several different shapes. Help the children to sort them into cuboids, cubes, triangular prisms, cylinders, square-based pyramids, etc. If you have enough boxes, set tasks such as, 'Make the highest wall you can using this shape.' Try stacking each shape in turn. If you have time, make cardboard cones with bases. Talk about tessellations and the interlocking patterns of house bricks.

Use small cardboard boxes to build a house large enough for the children to play in. Tissue boxes are ideal. Discuss the problems that arise, e.g. how to stick the boxes together; and use *Lego* to resolve any difficulties in design, e.g. constructing corners and lintels for doors. Let the children try to apply the solutions to the actual building.

Make a bird's nest

Collect the materials for a garden-bird's nest: twigs, roots, mud, feathers, wood shavings, dried grass, etc. If possible, let the children see an old nest and/or show them pictures. Then let them try to build a nest: they will soon discover how difficult this is, and birds use only their beaks and feet.

Make a wormery

Kits can be bought for this, or a parent may be able to make a simple wooden frame with two sheets of perspex slotted into grooves at the sides.

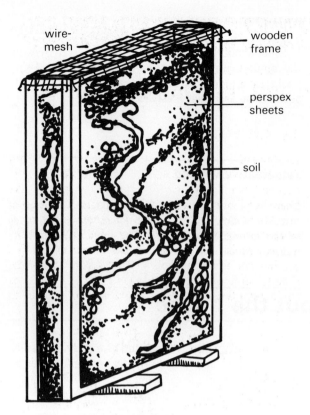

Fill the container with damp soil. Add three or four worms from the garden and leave the wormery in a dark place. Put a gauze top on to prevent escapes, and after a few days you should be able to observe a network of tunnels. Keep the soil moist and, once the observation is over, return the worms carefully to the garden. Involve the children in this so that they learn to value life.

Tunnels and burrows

Talk about animals that burrow and man-made tunnels (you could mention the Channel tunnel). Then ask the children to make a tunnel or burrow in the sand-tray, first in dry sand and then in damp sand. Offer them a variety of tools and scrap materials to help.

Make an underwater home

Discuss animal homes under water and the different structures used by humans to enable them to survive under water. For the investigation, provide the children with a large trough or tank of water, gravel and various containers. Ask them to make an underwater home for a water-dwelling creature, and then for an air-breathing creature. How can air be put into an underwater home? (Weight a bottle down on its side, using gravel, and blow bubbles of air into it through a plastic pipe.)

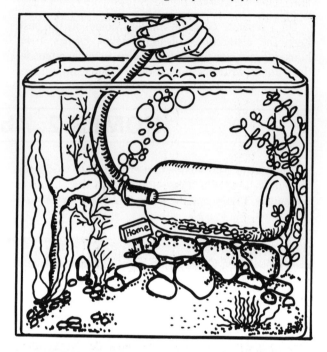

A model pit-dwelling

Early man dwelt in homes that were partly below ground level. Use reference books to find out more about these and about the associated way of life. Then help the children to construct such a home: dig a hole in soil held in a large container; and use stones, twigs, chamois leather and turf as shown in the diagram.

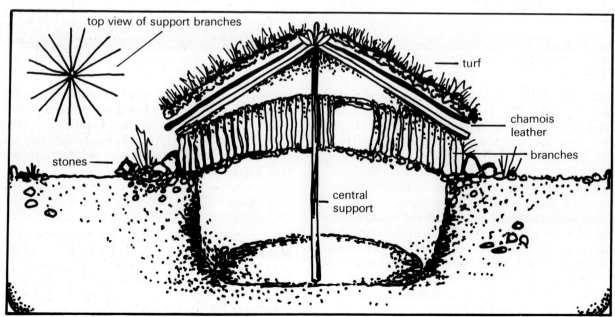

HOMES 4 and 5: Exterior and interior of a house

The children can colour the exterior of their house and design and colour the interior. To assemble, cut down the middle of sheet 4 (the exterior) and attach each half to sheet 5 (the interior) by the outer edges, either with glue or adhesive tape. The two halves can then be folded back to reveal the interior. Encourage individuality in decoration.

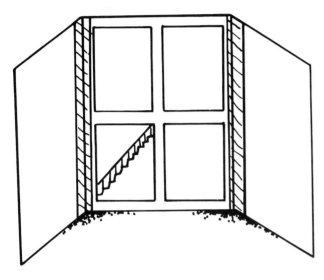

The finished houses can be displayed as detached homes, as 'semis', or as a terrace. Add trees, bushes, etc.

Fill in with a piece of roof.

Fill in.

Witch's house collage

Use a variety of scrap materials to make the witch's house from the story about Hansel and Gretel. Use sweet wrappings, bottle tops and can pulls, coloured paper, polystyrene shapes, bubble-prints (for candyfloss) and marbling (for toffee lollies) and make the collage as large as possible. To complete the scene add collage figures of the witch and the two children.

The Old Woman's shoe

Tell the children about the Old Woman who lived in a shoe and say that you are going to make a model of her strange home. Use boxes and wire netting to make the basic shoe shape, and cover this with tissue paper soaked in cold-water paste. When the model is dry, make, paint and put on a roof and windows and a door; and add shoe features such as a toe-cap, eyelets and the lace. The children could bring in dolls and stand them around the shoe to represent the Old Woman's children, and you could put a two-dimensional figure next to the shoe to represent the Old Woman herself.

Decorated clay tiles

Using self-hardening clay, roll out slabs of uniform thickness, either square or rectangular. The rectangular shapes can be decorated as kitchen or bathroom tiles, using impressed or applied-clay techniques, and then mounted as a brick-type tessellation.

The square tiles can be decorated to show the fronts of houses and displayed side by side as a ceramic frieze. Remember to make a hole in each while the clay is still soft, so that you can hang them on the wall.

Print your own wallpaper

Using potatoes, Plasticine® blocks or the faces of scrap items, print long strips of 'wallpaper'. Discuss use of colour, the size of design and, possibly, the room for which it is intended, e.g. fish for the bathroom. Let the children pick the design they like best and then you can mass-produce that one for the home corner.

Stained-glass windows

Cut a simple design out of two sheets of black activity paper. Then take tissue paper or coloured Cellophane®, and cut shapes slightly larger than the holes in the design. Glue these over the holes, sandwiching them between the two sheets of black paper to give a neat finish to both sides.

Weaving

Use cloth, paper or wool for this (see the topic *Clothes*). Discuss different uses of fabric in the home, e.g. for decoration, comfort, cleaning.

Make a model village

Use large flat tissue boxes as the base for homes (two for a house, one for a bungalow). Children can decorate models of their own homes, or the models might be linked to your reading materials or show houses through the ages. Straw can be stuck to the roof to represent thatch, and a whole village could be made showing different kinds of homes and other buildings.

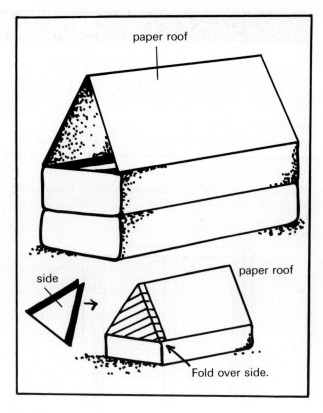

Rubbings

Using wax crayons, take rubbings from a variety of textured surfaces in the home, e.g. embossed wallpaper, brick walls, cord carpets, brocade curtains, bamboo placemats.

MUSIC

Sing songs about homes: 'No Place like Home'; 'Home on the Range'; 'Little Boxes'; 'The Wise Man built his House upon the Rocks'; 'This Old House'; 'In a Cottage in a Wood'.

DANCE, DRAMA AND PE

Set up a home corner and encourage various domestic role-play activities by providing equipment such as a toy iron, clothes, a table, a cooker. Act out the whole or part of *Hansel and Gretel*, or perhaps a nursery rhyme like 'There was an Old Woman'. You could build a cave in the corner of the classroom and give the children information about 'cavemen' so that they have a model for imaginative play.

Mime building a house: stacking bricks, sawing, hammering, carrying heavy weights, climbing ladders, painting. Then mime cleaning the house: washing, dusting, cleaning windows, sweeping. The mime can be linked to movement activities in PE: stretching, curling, bending, balancing. The children can work alone or with a partner to create interesting movement sequences, e.g. dig, stoop, lift, climb; dig, stoop, lift, climb; ...

RELIGIOUS EDUCATION

Look at places of worship and try to arrange visits to different ones, e.g. church, synagogue, mosque, temple, gurdwara. Stories from the Bible might include Noah's Ark; and the story of the Nativity, in which Mary and Joseph have nowhere to stay but a stable.

Talk about people and families who have no homes because of such things as famine, floods, drought, war, forest fires, earthquakes and volcanic activity. Discuss what we can do to help, and the work of big organisations like Unicef, Oxfam, Save the Children and Shelter.

Talk about habitats, human and animal. Look at the way houses have developed in different climatic regions and how the natural resources of the area influence their design, e.g. houses on stilts in areas of frequent flooding, igloos in polar regions.

Compare life in the country with life in a town. Look at homes through history, using books and filmstrips, and, if possible, visit an old building in the area. Look at animal homes and use books and videos to find out more about different habitats. Again, if possible, go out and look at animal homes, e.g. birds' nests, burrows, sets, and ponds, but be careful not to cause any disturbance.

HOMES 6: Animal habitats

This is a simple exercise linking some common animals with their homes and habitats. It will practise the children's skills of representational drawing to a given size (to fit the picture), and will extend their vocabulary.

Make friezes to show different animal and human homes around the world; you could make two separate friezes for each region or combine the facts, e.g. the polar frieze could show an igloo, a wooden stilt-house and a chalet for humans; and snow caves in which polar bears give birth, and the burrows of several small tundra-dwelling mammals. Try to show the variety of human dwellings in any one area, e.g. for China show the Imperial Palace, modern flats, shanty towns and simple village huts.

Instead of a frieze, you could show your pictures linked by string to the relevant regions on a large world map. Even infants will have seen TV pictures of Earth as seen from space, and they enjoy looking at maps and relating other countries to their own.

HOMES 7: Homes survey

If possible, use this record sheet during a class walk or outing; it should not be used by individuals or groups, as supervision is essential. If you can not take the children out, conduct a 'survey' of the buildings and homes shown in a book or series of books. You may need more than one copy of the sheet. A box is ticked for each 'sighting' in a category.

69

Human homes

Animal homes

About the house

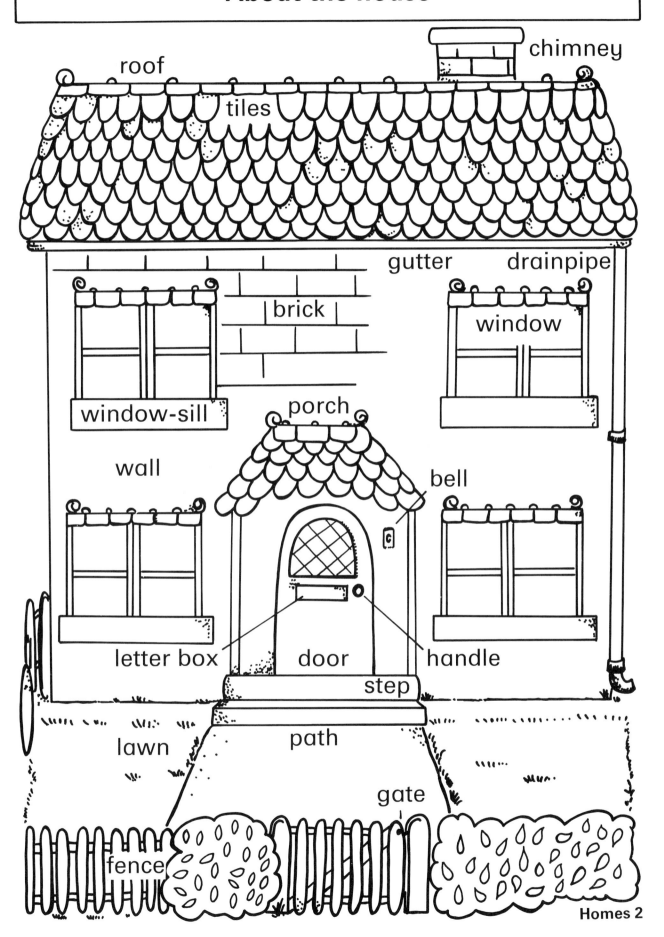

roof

tiles

chimney

gutter   drainpipe

brick

window

window-sill

porch

bell

wall

letter box   door   handle

step

lawn   path

gate

fence

Homes 2

71

Match the homes with the shapes.

Homes 4

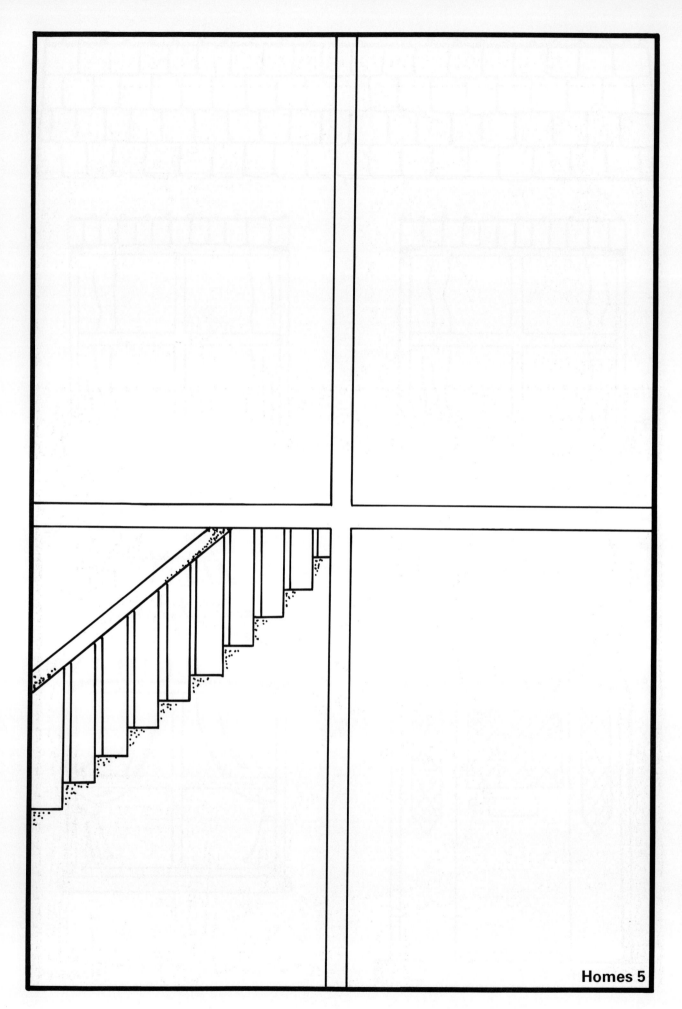

Homes 5

Draw each animal in its resting place.

trout

badger

crow

kingfisher

grey squirrel

spider

Homes 6

75

Homes survey

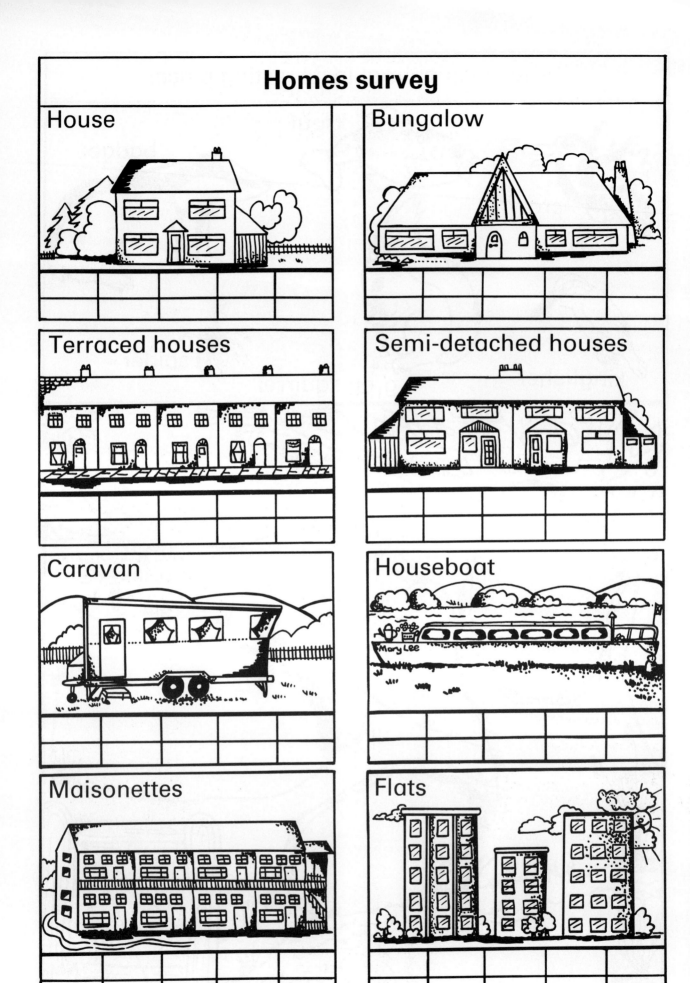

House

Bungalow

Terraced houses

Semi-detached houses

Caravan

Houseboat

Maisonettes

Flats

Homes 7

76

Mathematics NC Level 2 Core Subject

Pictographs. **AT 1, 9, 12, 13**
Order in dressing. **AT 1, 8, 9**
One-to-one matching. **AT 1, 9, 13**
Comparisons. **AT 1, 8, 9**

Science NC Level 2 Core Subject

Testing fabrics for insulation, absorption of heat and water, durability, waterproofing. **AT 1, 6, 9, 13**
Safety and clothes.

Art and craft

Spinning and weaving.
French knitting.
Sewing.
Wax-resist on fabrics.
Printing on fabrics.

Music

Listening to extracts from musicals.
Singing songs.

CLOTHES

Language NC Level 2 Core Subject
AT 1–5

Vocabulary exercises.
Factual writing about special clothes.
Reportive factual writing about experiments.
Imaginative writing.
Stories and poems.

Dance, drama and PE

Home corner role-play: a clothes shop.
Improvisation: clothes in a washing machine, on a line.

Religious education

Discussing stories: Joseph and The Emperor.
Talking and writing about pride, envy, greed and jealousy.

Environmental studies

Clothes in different cultures.
Clothes for different jobs and occasions.
Fashion.

CLOTHES

1 We wear clothes to keep us warm or cool or dry or safe.

2 Clothes are made of different materials which have different properties that help to keep us warm, cool, dry or safe.

3 Clothes can tell others what kind of job we do.

4 Clothes can tell others which country we come from.

5 We have clothes for different occasions.

STARTING POINT

Sort out the clothes in the home corner to make sure there are suitable sets for dressing up. Of course, if you don't have any dressing-up clothes, provide some: skirts, dresses, aprons, shawls, waistcoats, belts, scarves, trousers, etc. Pieces of net curtain and brocade will also be translated into garments by inventive infants. If possible, provide various fantasy/role-play outfits: cowboy, nurse, clown, prince, princess, soldier, policeman, policewoman, etc. Encourage the children to bring in My Little Pony®, Barbie® and Sindy® dolls, Action Man® – any toy that has a variety of outfits for different occasions (sport, entertainment or work). These can form the basis of a class display. Dolls in national costume would be colourful and meaningful additions to this.

Collect posters and pictures of clothes for different purposes, such as sporting events, relaxation, the arts (ballet and theatre costumes), uniforms and protection. These pictures can be mounted singly or as montage sets for class display. Ask the children to bring in items of clothing that their fathers or mothers wear, such as protective clothes, uniforms, leisurewear, etc.

Stories could include *The Emperor's New Clothes*, *Cinderella* and *The Elves and the Shoemaker*. Try to find poems about different clothes, and particularly good descriptions of them, to stimulate children's imaginations.

LANGUAGE

CLOTHES 1: Clothes for hot and cold days

Use this sheet as a language exercise and then, perhaps enlarged, as a vocabulary chart. Each half sheet could also be used with the other half 'blanked out' to make a page in a topic book. For the exercise, the children choose words from the given vocabulary. As an extension,

the children could write about the clothes they wear on a cold/hot day or an adventure they had in a cold/hot place. *Blueprints: Writing* in this series provides plenty of topic sheets suitable for imaginative writing.

CLOTHES 2: Special clothes

After discussion, the children can match each word to the correct box, using the initial letters as clues. When all the words have been placed, the children can draw themselves in appropriate clothes.

Other writing could include direct observations about the experiments in the section on science. Use these headings: *What we wanted to know; What we used; What we did; What we found out*. Factual writing could concern jobs which require a uniform or protective clothing; clothes worn in countries with climates different from our own; current fashions in contrast with what the children's parents wore as children and teenagers (photographic evidence will be needed here!). Imaginative writing could use the theme 'If I were a (deep-sea diver, ballet dancer, clown . . .)'.

MATHEMATICS

CLOTHES 3: Top-coat graph

Make a graph to show the different types of coat worn by the class on one day. When the children are lined up, count how many of the most popular type there are and then photocopy the sheet that many times. Cut up the sheets and, after a class discussion about the merits of each type of coat, give a picture of the appropriate coat to each child to colour. The coloured pictures can be made into a pictograph or sorted into sets for the properties of style and colour, e.g. blue anoraks, red ski-suits. As an alternative or extension activity, make a graph to show shoe size and colour, using cut-out pictures of the shoe styles worn by the class.

CLOTHES 4: Order in dressing

This sheet shows a set of unisex clothes. The children can colour them and then cut out the squares or the items, and stick them down in the order in which they are usually put on when dressing.

SCIENCE

Here are some simple experiments concerned with the properties of textiles and clothes.

Insulation

Use various materials, e.g. newspapers, blankets, coats. Wrap up three children, each one in *one* layer of *one* of the materials. Then wrap up three more children, each one in *several* layers of *one* of the materials. See how they feel after a few minutes, but don't let them get too hot. Ask them to describe how they feel to the other children. This should show that we keep warmer if we wear layers of clothing.

Some fabrics have built-in insulation, e.g. quilted or fur materials in which air is trapped. Submerge different fabrics in water and watch the air bubbles rise.

Discuss with the children which fabrics they think keep them warmest and collect pieces of those fabrics. Include a piece of tinfoil, a string vest and a nylon material. Borrow as many hot-water bottles as you have types of material, plus one, and fill each one with hot water (remember safety precautions). Wrap one hot-water bottle completely in each different material, leaving the last bottle unwrapped as a control, and see which ones cool quickest or slowest. You will need to decide whether or not your children can understand a timing device, and how to record results. Talk about things like gloves, scarves, ear-muffs and hats which we can add to our usual clothing to keep us extra warm.

Waterproofing

Some clothes are designed to keep us dry and we call these clothes *waterproof*. The children may wonder what it is that makes some clothes waterproof, and this could lead on to the testing of the fabrics from which raincoats, anoraks, cagoules, etc. are made.

To test for the property of being waterproof, collect a range of material samples and stretch each one across a clear plastic container. Using a dropper so that you can control the amount of water used, drop water onto each material in turn. Discuss with the children what happens: does the water run off? If not, how long before a drip passes through, and how many pass through? Which fabrics let the water pass through quickly? Out in the playground, the children can test their own raincoats with a watering can.

Try waterproofing a range of material samples by rubbing them with a candle or coating them with PVA glue or shoe polish. Test each treated material as described earlier and see if the 'waterproofing' has worked.

Absorbency

To test the rate at which different fabrics absorb water, set up the following experiment. Attach strips of different materials to a length of wood. Discuss with the children how long the pieces should be and if they should all be the same length. Let the end of each rest in a pot of water. Ask the children if there should be the same amount of water in each pot. Some children of this age can see that a race or a test should be the same for all the competitors and can transfer this principle to the experimental situation. Of course, if they cannot then simply say that you will make everything the same to make it fair.

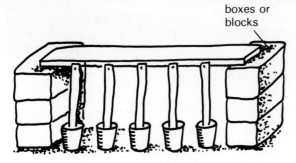

boxes or blocks

The children will be able to see how far up the pieces of material the water soaks, and put them in order (first, second, third, etc.) from most absorbent to least absorbent. Talk about clothes that need to be absorbent, e.g. sweatshirts and bathrobes.

After investigating waterproof and absorbent materials, talk about umbrellas and tents and how they keep us dry. Clearly, shape plays a part. Look at the shape of an umbrella and watch water running off its taut, sloped sides when it is open and off its slack, flattened shape when closed.

Drying properties

From previous experiments the children know that many materials can absorb and hold water. Many of them will know that their parents find this a problem when trying to dry clothes quickly.

Collect a range of materials or dolls' clothes made out of different materials and wash them. Hang them on a washing line outside on a windy or a sunny day and take careful note of when the clothes dry. Make a chart to show the order in which they dried. You could repeat the process after discussion with the children and introduce variables like not wringing the clothes before drying; or hanging out the washing on a very still, damp day. Then the children will discover some of the other factors concerned in drying, i.e. removing as much water as possible before pegging out and the effect of air that is moving and capable of absorbing water vapour (a dry wind).

CLOTHES 5: Which material dried quickest?

This sheet provides two ways in which the children can record what they find out about the drying properties of various materials. The top part of the sheet allows for recording results as a simple numerical order and should be within the capabilities of most children. The chart on the lower part of the sheet is for use by older children who are able to work out and record drying times. If you wish, you can blank out either half when photocopying, thus giving the children room to add their own comments.

Colour and absorption of heat

Clothes for warm weather are light and loose fitting and often light coloured. Discuss with the children the types of material used to make summer clothes.

Is colour important? These two simple experiments will help to show that dark colours absorb heat.

Choose a sunny window. Leave part of it uncovered; cover part with a square of black paper and another part with a square of white paper. After half an hour remove the papers and see which panes of glass feel hottest.

Let the children sit in a sunny window without curtains, then with a net curtain in place, and finally with a sheet of black card covering the window. Ask the children which covering let through most/least heat.

Durability

Talk about the clothes the children play in and how they get damaged: scuffed and torn trouser knees, torn skirts and shirts, frayed cuffs, worn elbows in shirts and blouses, holes in socks, and so on. Discuss which fabrics the children think would be suitable for rough wear. Would that material be suitable for, say, a pair of trousers or a boiler suit? Would it make good socks!

To test for damage through friction, collect a range of material samples about 30 cm square; and make a rough-play simulator by covering a hand-size block of wood with coarse sandpaper, or use part of a house brick. Fix each sample in turn to a block of wood or other board, perhaps with staples, and see what happens when you give it five rubs at a time with the simulator. Which fabric is the first to develop a hole? Which is the last?

CLOTHES 6: Which materials are hardwearing?

This sheet provides a means of recording the results of the previous investigation, and there is space also for the children's comments and opinions.

Flammability

Unfortunately many fabrics are highly flammable and many give off toxic fumes if burned, so we do not suggest you experiment in this area. However it is important to discuss the dangers and occasions when clothes might catch fire, e.g. bedclothes near an unguarded fire, long party dresses near a fire, play near a bonfire, when candles are in use. You could also discuss the potential dangers of other clothes, such as long scarves which might get trapped in bicycle wheels, untied shoe-laces which may cause a fall, and wearing purses on strings round the neck while playing. The children may be able to think of many more such dangers, and you could organise a competition to find the most effective warning-poster designs. Post the winning designs around the school.

Protective clothing

Collect pictures and photographs of protective clothing and, if possible, borrow actual examples of the clothes. Talk with the children about style and the fabrics used, in the light of what they have learned about the properties of various materials.

CLOTHES 7: Clothes for safety

Discuss with the children the various items of the fireman's clothing. The children should then be able to draw a line from each piece of equipment to the body part it is designed to protect.

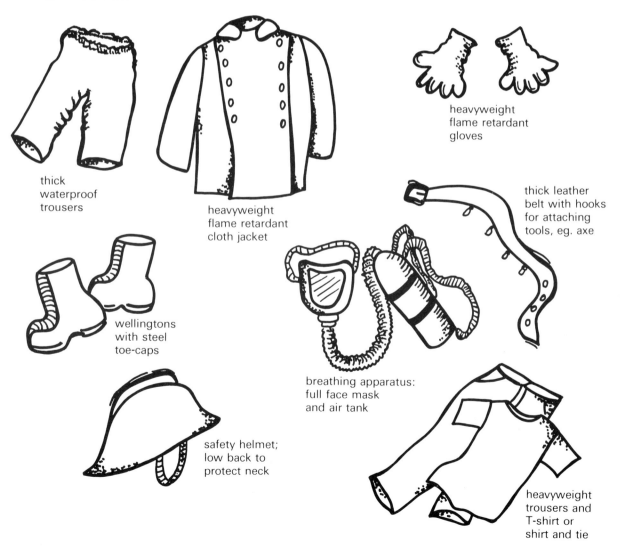

thick waterproof trousers

heavyweight flame retardant cloth jacket

heavyweight flame retardant gloves

thick leather belt with hooks for attaching tools, eg. axe

wellingtons with steel toe-caps

breathing apparatus: full face mask and air tank

safety helmet; low back to protect neck

heavyweight trousers and T-shirt or shirt and tie

Weaving

Look closely at the way in which woven fabrics are made. Use magnifying glasses or a microscope if you can. Then try to get hold of some unprocessed wool from sheep (in sheep-farming areas this is quite easy to obtain from fields and hedges). Wash the wool after collection and then it can be dyed with natural substances such as tea, coffee, onion skins, blackberries, beetroot, saffron, etc. Darker shades require more of the dyeing medium, and remember that wool always dries to a paler colour.

Let the children try to spin the wool with adult help. A visit to a craft centre would be a great incentive here if the children were able to see the spinning process before having a go themselves.

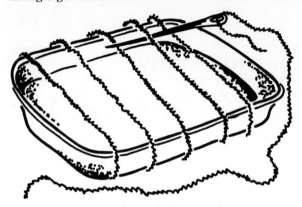

A simple first loom can be made from a polystyrene carton. These are particularly useful since there is a gap below the wool and the children have less difficulty in manipulating the needle under and over the threads.

Paper weaving is a simple alternative but almost any material can be used.

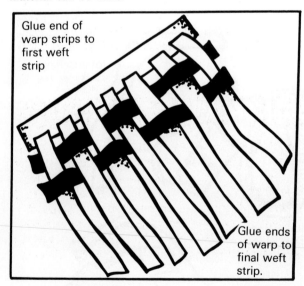

Glue end of warp strips to first weft strip

Glue ends of warp to final weft strip.

French knitting

This can be done by most children of this age group. All that is needed is a wooden cotton reel with four small nails in the top. The wool is wrapped around the nails as shown, then the loops are lifted over each nail in turn and the length of knitting is pulled down through the centre of the reel. The end-product is a long tube of knitted wool that can be made into mats, bags or hats.

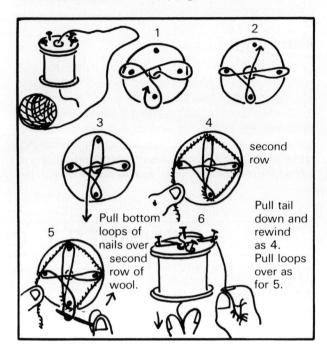

1

2

3

4

second row

Pull bottom loops of nails over second row of wool.

5

6

Pull tail down and rewind as 4. Pull loops over as for 5.

Sewing

Sewing cards followed by simple embroidery on Binca® is a good introduction to sewing. Then use felt to make a small purse or case as an introduction to the sewing together of two pieces of material. To follow this, dolls' clothes can be made in felt (see diagram of a simple pattern for a doll's dress/coat).

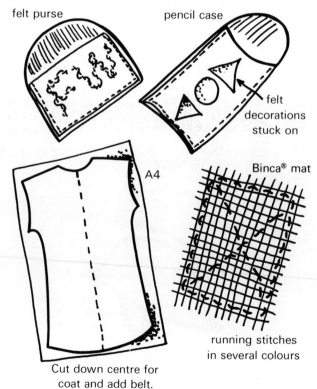

felt purse

pencil case

felt decorations stuck on

Binca® mat

A4

running stitches in several colours

Cut down centre for coat and add belt.

Patterns on fabrics

Wax-resist patterns
If possible, use plain white or very light material and be careful to fix it so that it is drawn taut, otherwise it will be difficult to draw on. Draw your pattern or design using wax crayons, and then dye the material with cold-water dyes. Dry flat and do not iron. To display, stretch the fabric over a board. A batik effect can be achieved by crumpling the waxed material prior to dyeing. It is important that the design is very heavily waxed, because the crumpling must crack the wax without ruining the design. After dyeing and drying, wash the material in hot water to remove the wax and reveal a pattern of fine lines where the dye seeped through the cracks. True batik requires hot wax, but that is too dangerous for use with infants.

Printing
Use potatoes or lumps of Plasticine® as printing blocks. Infants can use pencils to make interesting designs on the Plasticine®, but they will need adult help to 'carve' their potatoes, as sharp implements are involved. Keep the material taut when printing and make sure the block is well covered (but not dripping) with paint for each application.

MUSIC

Listen to extracts from *Joseph and the Amazing Technicolour Dreamcoat* (especially the title song); and *The Emperor's New Clothes*, sung by Danny Kaye. You could also learn songs like 'Soldier, Soldier, Won't You Marry Me?' and 'My Hat it has Three Corners'.

DANCE, DRAMA AND PE

Turn the home corner into a clothes shop by providing racks, a 'till' and money, and various articles of clothing and/or pieces of material.

In drama and PE sessions the children can pretend to be clothes in a washing machine or blowing on a line: this will develop their vocabulary of movement with words such as twisting, stretching, curling, jumping, flapping. They can also pretend to be wearing strange clothes and move appropriately, e.g. a suit of armour, heavy boots, a suit covered with flying balloons, a long cloak or dress, magic flying boots.

RELIGIOUS EDUCATION

Read the stories of Joseph and his coat of many colours and *The Emperor's New Clothes*, and talk about feelings of pride, greed, jealousy and envy. The children could then write about one of those emotions and illustrate their writing with a picture of Joseph or the Emperor. In discussion, help the children to appreciate that it is the person who wears the clothes that is important, not the clothes themselves. Encourage understanding of and respect for people who wear special clothes for ethnic or religious reasons.

ENVIRONMENTAL STUDIES

Discuss the clothes that we wear in school for special occasions: T-shirts and shorts for PE, painting overalls, football kit, swimming costumes, clothes for assemblies and plays, dressing-up clothes, aprons for cooking, and the school uniform (if there is one).

Look around for examples of ethnic dress in the neighbourhood and invite members of ethnic groups to come into school and talk about their clothes, e.g. how to put on a sari, why turbans are worn and how they are put on.

Collect pictures of the clothes commonly worn by different peoples around the world and compare typical 'western' dress with some of the others, e.g. Arabian, Masai, Indian, Finnish. If possible, borrow examples of national and folk costumes (real clothes or on dolls).

Discuss current fashions and those of the recent past. You should be able to obtain photographs and/or pictures which will amuse and stimulate the children.

Clothes for hot and cold days

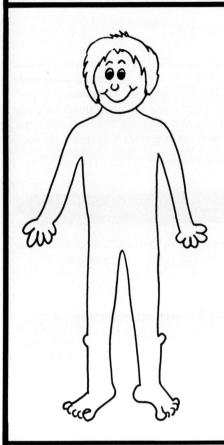

These are some of the things that help to keep us cool.

On this figure, draw the things that **you** might wear or use on a hot day.

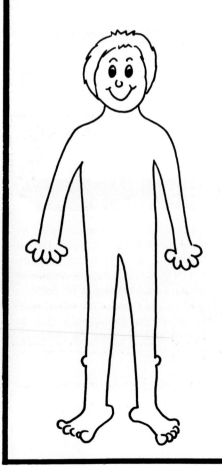

These are some of the things that help to keep us warm.

On this figure, draw the things that **you** might wear on a cold day.

Clothes 1

84

Special clothes

Fill in the missing letters and draw the pictures.

| p | | | | | |

| w | | | | | | | |

| s | | | | | | |

| s | | | | | | |

| h | | | | |

| f | | | | | | | | |

| r | | | | | |

| m | | | | | |

wedding   party   skiing   swimming

football match   horse riding

Clothes 3

86

Put these clothes in order for dressing.

Clothes 4

Which material dried quickest?

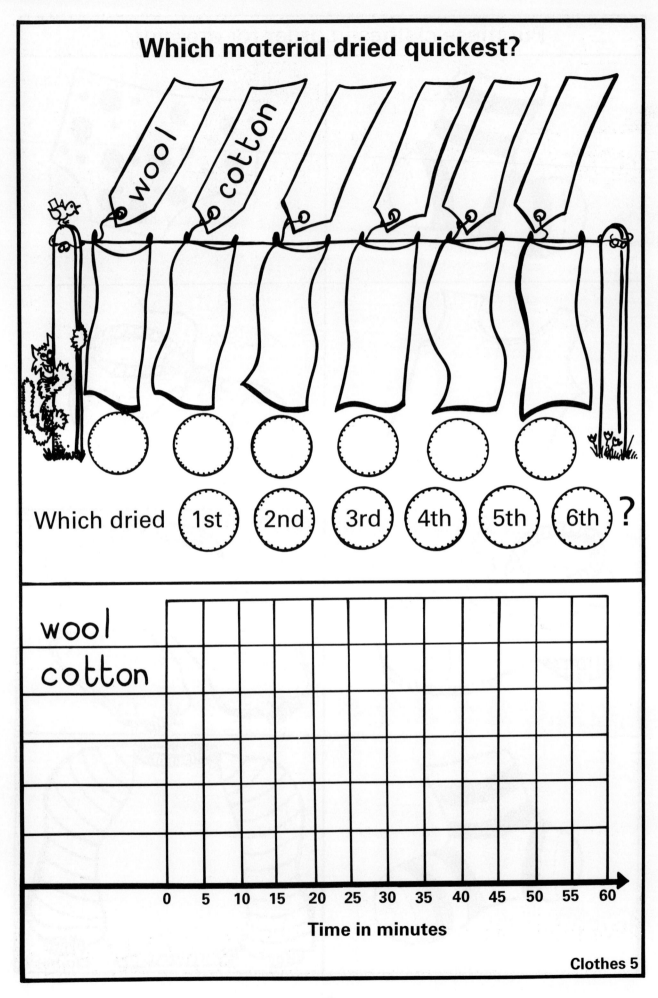

wool   cotton

Which dried (1st) (2nd) (3rd) (4th) (5th) (6th) ?

wool												
cotton												

0   5   10   15   20   25   30   35   40   45   50   55   60

Time in minutes

Clothes 5

88

Which materials are hardwearing?

Is [   ] hardwearing material?

We rubbed it with sandpaper to find out.

After 5 rubs we noticed _____

_____

After 10 rubs we noticed _____

_____

After 15 rubs we noticed _____

_____

After 20 rubs we noticed _____

_____

We think this material is/is not hardwearing.

Clothes 6

Dress the fireman to keep him safe.

Clothes 7

Mathematics NC Level 3 Core Subject

Handling money; tickets. **AT 1, 8, 9**
Revision of time; using
  timetables; the 24-hour
  clock. **AT 1, 8, 9**
The relationship between
  distance, speed and
  journey time. **AT 1, 8, 9**
Comparisons. **AT 1, 8, 9**

Science NC Level 3 Core Subject

Experiments: air power;
  momentum and inertia;
  stored energy; water power. **AT 1, 10, 13**
Other power sources in transport. **AT 1, 9**
Strength in paper structures. **AT 1, 6**
Design in vehicles: hulls, sails, etc. **AT 1, 6**
Vehicles in the future.

Art and craft

Prints and patterns with
  items of machinery.
3D collage.
Photo-montage.
Junk vehicles.
Model hot-air balloon.
Kites.
Wall-pictures and friezes.

Music

Listening to music.
Learning and singing songs.
Use of non-tuned percussion
  instruments for rhythms
  and transport noises.

TRANSPORT

Language NC Level 3 Core Subject
AT 1–5

Stories and topic books.
Reportive writing about the
  children's own research
  and experiments.
Imaginative writing.
Vocabulary charts and a
  crossword puzzle.

Dance, drama and PE

Role-play in the home corner.
Drama: acting as a passenger
  or member of staff in various
  forms of transport; waiting
  in a queue; driving in a traffic-
  jam; stuck at an airport; etc.
Movement: contrasts like starting
  and stopping. Group work –
  moving as a machine.

Religious education

Biblical and other
  stories; the journey
  through life.

Environmental studies

History of transport.
Vehicles for specific purposes.
Animal-powered transport.
Your local area: map and
  traffic survey.
Transport around the world.
Transport and hobbies.
Transport and communication.

TRANSPORT

BASIC CONCEPTS

1 Transport means to *carry across*.

2 We can travel through the air, on the water, under-water, over land and underground.

3 All vehicles are powered by some form of energy.

4 Most land vehicles have wheels or tracks.

5 Most air vehicles have wings or fins. Balloons are an exception.

6 Most water transport floats on the surface. Submarines are an exception.

STARTING POINT

Go for a walk down the road from school and see how many different vehicles you can spot. Go for a bus, train or ferry ride; and visit the bus station, railway station, ferry or air terminal, or a port or dockyard.

There are railway, maritime and general transport museums in all parts of the country today, and these would provide useful stimulus for this topic. Agricultural shows, too, exhibit many different types of farm vehicles. The major commercial shows such as the Boat Show, the Motor Show and various air shows would also, of course, be interesting, if you can arrange a visit.

Collect books on all aspects of transport, including space. Watch video extracts from films like *Herbie, Those Magnificent Men in their Flying Machines*, and *Chitty, Chitty, Bang Bang*.

Children can bring in their own model cars, boats, planes and trains. A road playmat will stimulate a great deal of play with these toys, and may spark off some interesting questions. Construction kits like *Lego*, and wooden building bricks can be used to build airports, motorways, etc.

Read poems on the subject, e.g. Robert Louis Stevenson's *View from a Railway Carriage*; and stories such as *Thomas the Tank Engine, Ivor the Engine, Postman Pat, Fireman Sam, The Railway Children* (E. Nesbit), *Twenty Thousand Leagues under the Sea* (Jules Verne), *Pegasus the Flying Horse*, and *The Wishing Chair* (Enid Blyton). The James Bond films show many imaginative forms of transport.

LANGUAGE

Listen to and read appropriate stories and gather information from topic books, starting wherever the children are most interested. You can teach research skills at this stage by providing simple workcards to focus the children's attention on certain parts of books. Show them again how to use the contents, index and glossary. The children can discuss what they have found out and do reportive writing on any aspect you choose. They can also write up what they find out when doing the science experiments.

TRANSPORT 1: Different sorts of transport

This sheet can be used as the cover for a topic booklet; for factual writing; and, enlarged, as a class vocabulary sheet. In the latter instance, include words the children come across in their research, e.g. *arrival, departure, speed, tunnel, bridge*.

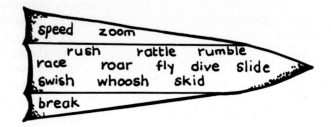

speed zoom
rush rattle rumble
race roar fly dive slide
swish whoosh skid
break

TRANSPORT 2: You and a clue

This crossword reinforces common words from the vocabulary of transport, but it is quite sophisticated in its presentation. Start the children off with something simpler if necessary, or let them work in pairs or groups.

TRANSPORT 3: Pegasus

Tell the children the story of Pegasus the winged horse and then let them write it in their own words. Alternatively, the children can invent their own stories of a flying horse; the sheet has no title so the children can invent their own.

Other topics for imaginative writing include *The enchanted train, A day out, Special machine, Journey into space, The magic carpet.* Also ideas such as *The mad inventor, Time traveller, If I could fly, Transport of the future* will provoke a lot of discussion and some interesting written work.

MATHEMATICS

Set up the home corner as a ticket office or an airport terminal and give the children experience of handling money. Collect as many different types of timetable as you can, from railway and bus stations and travel agents. You can also obtain advertising posters, which may give extra information and will certainly add to the atmosphere, as will a large map of the British Isles. Let the children make and 'buy' tickets to wherever they like.

Using the timetables, revise concepts of time: days of the week and months; and writing dates as a series of numbers, e.g. 9/9/1999 or 9.9.1999 or even 9.9.99. With able children you may be able to use the 24-hour clock to work out journey times. If necessary employ simple workcards, e.g. 'The train left at 3 p.m. and arrived at 7 p.m. How long did the journey take?' Or 'The train left at 03.00 and arrived at 07.00. How long did the journey take?'

On a simple outline map of the British Isles, mark your home town and various large cities and well-known places. Use the timetables and a teaching clock to work out journey times from your home town to different places. Record the times on the map. Record distances as well; and introduce the relationship between speed and time and distance by talking about how fast the children think a plane, a train, a car, a bike . . . can travel.

SCIENCE

The activities and experiments described here deal with various forms of 'transport' and look at their design and the source of power employed.

Air power

To demonstrate the power of moving air, blow up balloons and then let them go. The escaping air will send the balloons all over the room at a great rate and illustrate the element of thrust in a jet engine.

Make a hovercraft

Make a small hole in the bottom of a margarine tub and push the end of a balloon through this, as shown. Blow up the balloon and, holding the end, turn the tub over a smooth, flat surface. Release the balloon end and the 'hovercraft' should skim across the surface until the power source is exhausted.

Blow.

Design a glider

Flight through air power requires uplift. Talk about how gliders fly, using the uplift of thermal air currents to stay up in the air. But remember that gliders need the thrust power of another vehicle to launch them.

Find out how well different paper gliders fly – test these designs and any others that you or the chldren can devise. Can the children identify any aspects of design that particularly affect performance?

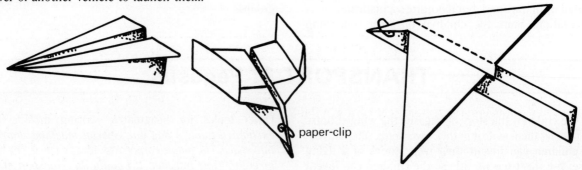

paper-clip

TRANSPORT 4: Template for glider

The template can be cut out as indicated and then folded along the lines in the order shown, taking care to crease sharply.

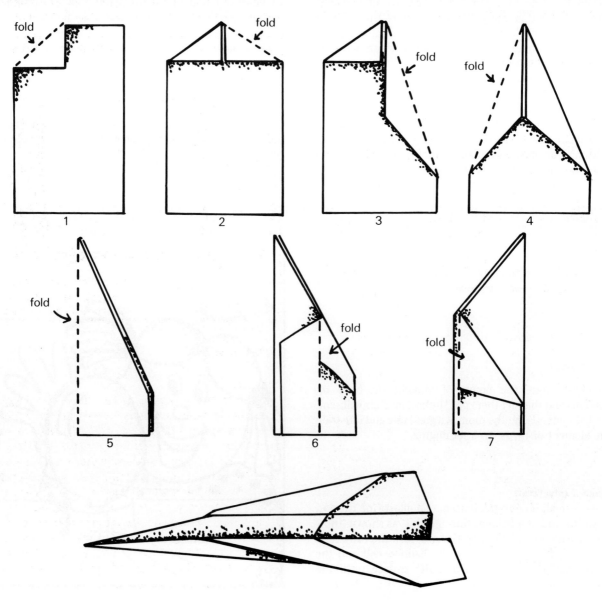

Make a parachute
Take a piece of cloth about the size of a man's hankie and tie a fine string to each corner. Add a weight or a plastic toy figure, throw the whole thing up in a ball and see how it lands. Now cut a small hole in the centre of the square and see if it falls in a different manner. See, too, if the length of the strings has any effect. You can also try using different sized cloths, because the air pushing upwards into the fabric slows the descent.

TRANSPORT 5: Car trials

This experiment is concerned with momentum and inertia and the sheet provides a means of recording the effect of slope on the distance travelled by a toy car or cars. You will need a toy car to which you can easily add or remove masses (weights) or two cars of obviously different masses. Use a piece of wood or stiff cardboard as a ramp and vary the angle of slope by using 1/2/3 house or wooden bricks. Record the distances travelled by colouring the 50 cm blocks on the sheet (you will need two sheets if two cars are tested). The actual measurement should be written on the number line, above the point where the colour recording stops.

Allow the children to test the range of variables suggested at the bottom of the sheet and record their results in the spaces provided. Use a sandpaper covering to make the ramp rough-surfaced.

Using stored energy

Make a paddle-boat
You will need a matchbox, two used matches, a small rubber band and a piece of card. Construct the boat as shown and try it out.

The thrust here is similar to that of a propeller, although

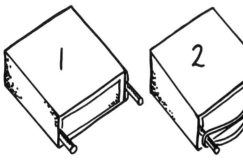

Position the two used matches.

Stretch the rubber band between them.

Use a piece of card as a paddle.

Use the paddle to wind up the band.
Put the boat in water.

the screw's effect is more powerful. If possible, show the children pictures of old paddle-driven riverboats and a modern screw-type propeller. Test other water toys that have propellers, and find out about how many forms of transport, in and out of water, are moved by a propeller. The stored energy in our experiment is, of course, in the rubber band.

Make a cotton-reel tank
This works on the same principle as the boat, but the matchstick is prevented from going round by the floor so it transfers its energy to the reel, which behaves like a wheel. Talk about which vehicles have wheels. Are wheels suitable on every terrain? You could hold 'tank' races on various surfaces to see whose tank travels furthest.

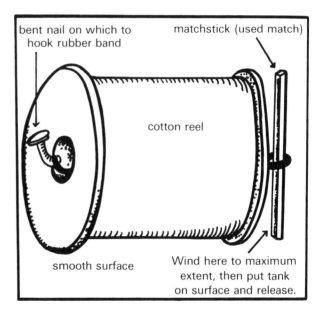

bent nail on which to hook rubber band

matchstick (used match)

cotton reel

smooth surface

Wind here to maximum extent, then put tank on surface and release.

Water power

Buoyancy
Using a large trough of water, test a selection of things for floating and sinking. Include various metal objects. Then see if a large metal dish/pan will float (choose a pan appropriate to the depth of the water so that it will float). The children are bound to ask why the dish floats when metal itself sinks in other forms. The answer is that the dish, in an upright position, offers to the water a surface on which the water can push to an extent (or force) equal to the mass of the water displaced by the dish. So the dish floats, like a boat. However, if you tip the dish sideways, the water has nothing much to push against and the dish will slide beneath the surface and sink, as does a capsized boat.

Make Plasticine® boats

These need careful moulding and handling, but will float successfully. Try out various shapes for the hull – which enable the boats to move through the water more easily?

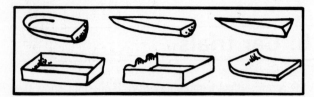

Introduce the idea of a keel to make the boats more stable, and then make sails (with drinking straws and paper). Try out various shapes of sail: rectangular, square, circular, triangular; and discuss with the children how to produce a steady 'wind'. They could blow on the boat or use paper fans or bicycle pumps. What about an empty plastic squeezy bottle, or a hair-dryer (held by an adult)?

Note: The topic *Water* includes experiments to show the power that comes from water and steam.

Make a steam turbine

This experiment must be treated as a demonstration and be conducted by the teacher, with full safety precautions. You will need a large metal can, or old pan, with a hole in the lid.

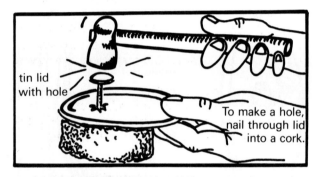

tin lid with hole

To make a hole, nail through lid into a cork.

Fix a vertical support to each side of the can and connect these at the top by a wire rod supporting a foil wheel (like the water-wheel described on page 51). Place the can, part filled with water, on a secure support over a

heat source. When the water boils and steam begins to escape from the hole in the lid, the wheel will start to spin. Remember that the can/pan will remain hot for some time and that the wheel will become very hot as well. Beware of the water boiling away.

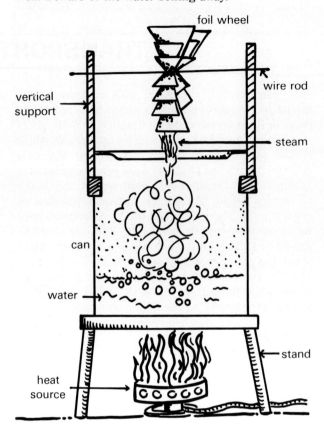

foil wheel

wire rod

vertical support

steam

can

water

heat source

stand

Other activities

Try to discover how many sources of power are employed in transport of all kinds (don't forget the power of animals, including humans). The experiment about moving a heavy object with the help of rollers is relevant here (see page 36).

Use junk materials, wooden building blocks and rolls of paper to construct bridges. Test their strength, taking care that there is no chance of a heavy mass falling on anyone's toes!

ART AND CRAFT

Prints and patterns

Use cogs, wheels, rollers and other items from constructional kits as objects with which to print with thick paint on coloured paper. Dip the wheels of toy cars in poster paint and simply run the cars over paper in various ways.

3D collage

On a base of soft wood, polystyrene or cork tiles, let the children make collage designs using bits of old clocks, torches, etc.

Photo-montage

Collect photos of vehicles for cutting out and mounting. You can make a general montage, or choose a theme: cars, planes, ships, etc; land, sea, air; trains past and present; underground travel; and so on. Travel agents, sales rooms, transport magazines, car manufacturers and British Rail are all good sources of information and photographs.

A model hot-air balloon

Blow up a large round balloon and paste over it several layers of thin paper or tissue. When this is firm and dry, paint and later varnish or paint the model with PVA glue. Add woollen 'ropes' and a paper basket, painted plastic tub or small fruit or vegetable basket; and suspend the model from the ceiling on invisible thread.

Glue string onto top of balloon.

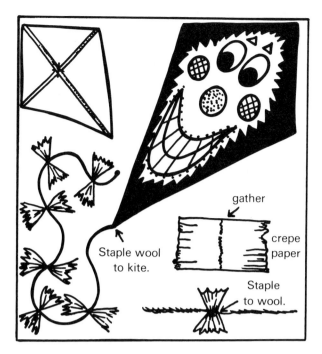

gather

crepe paper

Staple wool to kite.

Staple to wool.

Kites

Use newspaper spills or light canes for the skeleton and cover this with cartridge paper. Paint a design on the kite and then put a layer of PVA glue on both sides, for durability. The kite's tail can be made from wool with crepe-paper bows.

Wall-pictures and friezes

Make a collage frieze of animal-powered transport: husky dogs drawing sledges, camels, horses, llamas, donkeys, elephants, buffalo, etc. Try to use material that is representative of the animals' skins, and in the background show the appropriate environment. Discuss why a sleigh is better as a means of transport over snow than a wheeled vehicle.

A regatta is a splendid subject for a large wall-picture. Show different types of boat with sails of various colours against an azure sky and sapphire sea. This will give maximum illustrative effect of the fun of sailing.

MUSIC

Listen to music such as The Royal Scot; the themes from *The Orient Express* and *Chitty, Chitty, Bang Bang*; 'I Am Sailing'; 'Up, Up and Away'; 'Messing about on the River'; and 'Yellow Submarine'. The children will also enjoy learning these songs. Listen to the rhythm of R.L. Stevenson's *View from a Railway Carriage*. Use non-tuned percussion instruments to make different sounds: a jet engine, sails flapping, a car engine, a train, a tug chugging, a sleigh swishing through snow, a galloping horse.

DANCE, DRAMA AND PE

Turn the home corner into an airport terminal, a bus, a train, an airliner, a space rocket or a passenger liner and let the children role play spontaneously. Provide 'props' like tickets, silver-foil, switches, trays, plastic cups and saucers and rugs.

For more formal drama children can pretend they are in a ship, on a train, on an escalator, in a rocket, on an elephant, waiting in a queue, getting on a bus while carrying the shopping. Explore what it might be like to be a driver in a traffic jam, to miss a train, or be delayed at an airport.

In movement sessions explore contrasts: stopping and starting; slow steady movements and quick jerks; gliding and hovering or landing. Talk about how engines and other machines work; you may even be able to watch one moving. Notice how the parts move co-operatively. Start children off individually as cogs, wheels, pulleys, levers, etc. Then let them work in pairs, and finally in larger groups as big machines. The first child's movement could cause the second child's movement, and so on.

RELIGIOUS EDUCATION

There are many stories about journeys, in the Bible and in the scriptures of other religions. Traditional tales often have powerful moral implications about the journey through life – and these can be fun, they need not be didactic.

TRANSPORT 6: Noah's Ark

This sheet will be useful in other topics, as the story of Noah features in them as well. The children write the tale on the Ark, and then they can colour the picture. You may be able to devise similar sheets for other well-known stories: the tortoise and the hare (more haste, less speed); Apollo and the sun chariot (bringing dawn each day); Icarus (pride comes before a fall); the journey of Mary and Joseph to Bethlehem with Mary riding on a donkey.

ENVIRONMENTAL STUDIES

There are plenty of lines for study. Find out more about:

● The history of various forms of transport.
● Animal-powered transport around the world, and display the results pictorially in combination with a world map.
● Communication in transport: signs and signals, radio, TV, radar, sonar.
● Vehicles which help us: fire-engines, ambulances, break-down services, police cars, travelling medical and information services. You may be able to get one of these to visit your school. This category could include tugs and lifeboats as well.
● Service vehicles: refuse collectors, Post Office vans, street cleaners, snow ploughs, sand spreaders, steam-rollers and cranes.
● Commercial vehicles like delivery vans and lorries, removal vans, milk floats, ice-cream vans and hot-dog sellers.
● Vehicles which transport animals and people: buses, trains, taxis, boats, ferries, planes, hovercraft, barges, horse-boxes, caravans, and so on.

TRANSPORT 7: A traffic survey

Conduct and supervise a survey of traffic in your area, possibly outside the school, and record the results on this sheet by tallying. Individuals or groups of children can be made responsible for recording particular categories; empty spaces are available for noting unusual vehicles. Display the final results as a graph.

Make your own map

Provide a basic map of your area and let the children put in interesting landmarks, their own homes, and the things that they notice on their journeys to school.

Safety

Study *The Highway Code* and learn the Green Cross Code. Try to arrange for children with bikes to attend cycling proficiency lessons and take the test. Discuss drinking and driving: although the children do not drive themselves, they may be able to influence others positively and they can draw posters about the awful results. Take the opportunity to warn again about 'stranger danger' and stress that children must not get into any strange car or lorry. Find out about the work of the RNLI, the Coastguard and the air-sea rescue service.

Transport and fun

Investigate some of the many hobbies associated with vehicles: gliding, flying, ballooning, boating, sailing, water skiing, canoeing, cycling, motor cycling. What strange rides can the children think of, maybe at the fair?

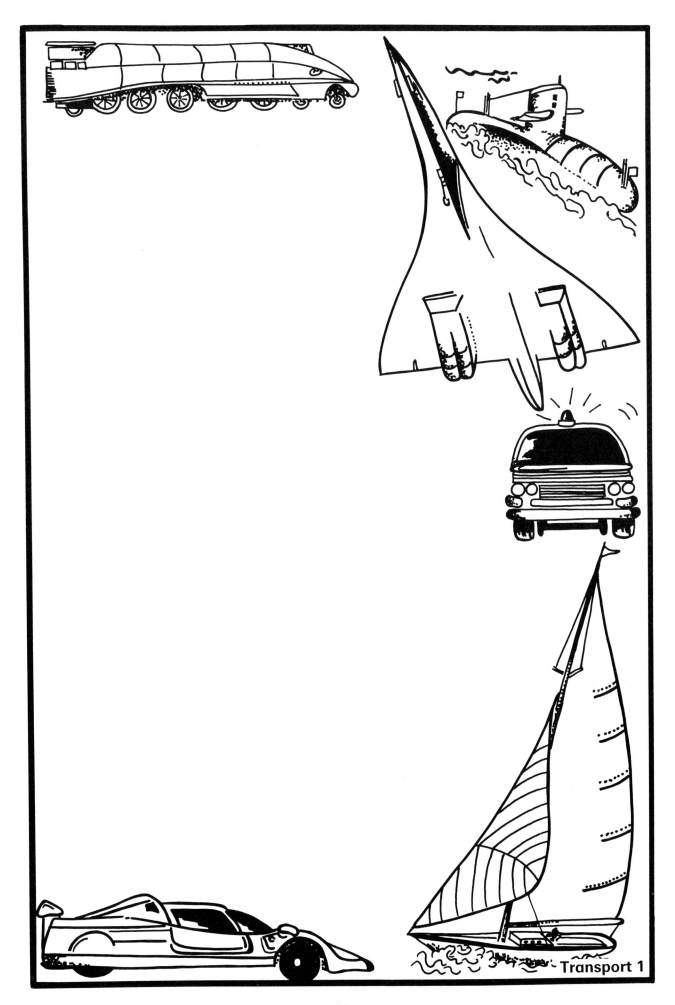

Transport 1

You and a clue

Clues

Across

3 Some children come to school on a b _ _.

4 A t _ _ _ _ moves on rails.

7 A h _ _ _ _ _ _ _ _ _ has blades on top.

10 A c _ _ has four wheels.

11 You start the e _ _ _ _ _ with a key.

Down

1 An a _ _ _ _ _ _ _ _ flies in the sky.

2 A train can r _ _ on rails.

3 A b _ _ _ has two wheels.

5 A s _ _ _ can cross the sea.

6 A g _ _ _ _ _ flies but has no engine.

8 A boat or a plane can carry a c _ _ _ _.

9 Cars and lorries travel on a r _ _ _.

Transport 2

Transport 3

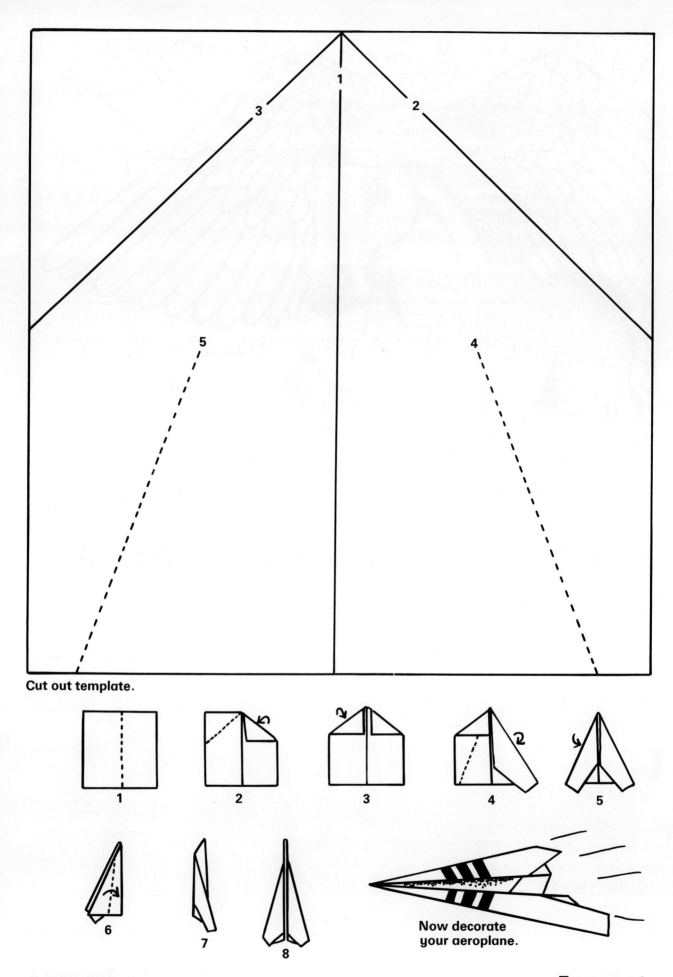

Cut out template.

1   2   3   4   5

6   7   8

Now decorate
your aeroplane.

Transport 4

102

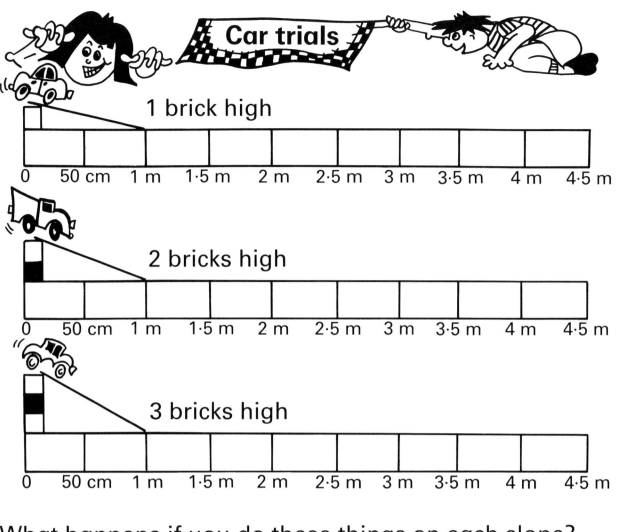

Car trials

1 brick high

| 0 | 50 cm | 1 m | 1·5 m | 2 m | 2·5 m | 3 m | 3·5 m | 4 m | 4·5 m |

2 bricks high

| 0 | 50 cm | 1 m | 1·5 m | 2 m | 2·5 m | 3 m | 3·5 m | 4 m | 4·5 m |

3 bricks high

| 0 | 50 cm | 1 m | 1·5 m | 2 m | 2·5 m | 3 m | 3·5 m | 4 m | 4·5 m |

What happens if you do these things on each slope?

1 Add a weight to the car. _____

_____

2 Use a ramp 50 cm long. _____

_____

3 Use a lighter car. _____

_____

4 Make the surface of the ramp rough. _____

_____

Transport 5

103

Noah's Ark

Our traffic survey

car	bicycle	bus

coach	lorry	articulated lorry

tanker	delivery van	small van

milk float	tractor	motorbike

police car	fire engine	ambulance

caravan	dormobile	
		Transport 7

105

Mathematics NC Level 3 Core Subject

Counting-on game. **AT 1, 2, 9**
Measuring lengths
(root and shoot growth)
and graphing results. **AT 1, 8, 9, 12, 13**

Science NC Level 3 Core Subject

Building a tunnel. **AT 1, 6**
Setting up a wormery,
an ant 'town', a
gerbil tank. **AT 1, 2**
Growing things without
soil; root systems. **AT 1, 2, 3**
Making lifting gear. **AT 1, 10, 13**

Art and craft

Wax rubbings. Brass rubbing.
Quilling, tube sculpture and
cardboard collage.
Clay work: thumb-pots.
Free painting, painting caves
and cave paintings.
Making and displaying jewellery.

Music

Listening to music.
Making echoes, and
echo-effects by
singing rounds.

UNDERGROUND

Language NC Level 3 Core Subject
AT 1–5

Discussion and early
research/reference skills.
Vocabulary collection.
Reportive writing about
experiments; an
underground trip.
Imaginative writing: various
approaches.
Poems. Crosswords.

Dance, drama and PE

Mime: actions in underground
work, and animals.
Imaginative play: home
corner as a prehistoric cave.

Religious education

Burial customs.
Monuments.
The raising of Lazarus.
The resurrection of Christ.

Environmental studies

Looking for holes that
lead underground.
Underground transport.
History of mining.
Fossils.

UNDERGROUND

BASIC CONCEPTS

1 There are many holes and tunnels in the earth's crust. Some are made by the actions of water, wind and heat, and by earth movements; others are made by animals or humans.

2 Animals and humans can live, work and travel underground.

3 We get fuel from underground (gas, coal, oil and hot water).

4 Most plants need an underground root system in order to grow.

STARTING POINT

Try to arrange a visit that takes you underground. You could explore a cellar; go for a walk to look at road excavations or pipe-laying work; travel by tube train; go for a train ride through a tunnel; take a canal-boat trip through a tunnel; visit a series of caves such as the Blue John Caverns in Derbyshire or Wookey Hole near Cheddar in Somerset; or visit a mining Heritage centre, such as Wigan Pier, to see how children were used in the mines in Victorian times (the Pier has a stretch of coalmine for you to walk through).

If possible, borrow a pair of gerbils and house them in a large glass aquarium with a wire-mesh lid. Fill this three-quarters full with soil and watch them burrow. (See DES and LEA rules for keeping animals in school.)

Collect posters and topic books with good illustrations and a suitable reading level. Areas of interest could include: animal homes underground, volcanoes, mining,

prehistoric animals, fossils, precious metals, caves and caving, pulleys and levers, excavation equipment, underground transport, tunnels, storage underground (vaults), geysers, oil, coal, gas, underground pipes and cables (water, phone, electricity, gas, sewers, etc.).

Stories and videos could be selected from *Journey to the Centre of the Earth* (Jules Verne); *Watership Down* (Richard Adams); the first part of *Alice in Wonderland* (Lewis Carroll); *The Minotaur*; the chapters on volcanoes from *The Living Planet* (David Attenborough).

Contact The Coal Board and various oil companies, some of whom provide posters, educational materials, slides and even videos about coal, oil and gas production.

Look at famous collections of jewels (or pictures of them), for example the Crown Jewels. Set up a treasure chest of sparkling costume jewellery.

LANGUAGE

Let the children look through a selection of topic books and then discuss with them what they have found out about underground things. This may encourage the children to find their own starting point, if one aspect interests them more than others at this stage.

Use the topic books to introduce simple research skills. You may find it useful to write out a set of workcards with basic questions; the children can then work alongside you, using contents and index pages to help them to find the answers. Simple group headings might be:

1 Animals underground
2 Transport
3 Fuels, precious metals and stones
4 Volcanoes, caves and geysers

The work can be done on a rotating group-work basis so that, over a period of weeks, the whole class has a chance to look at the various aspects of the topic.

UNDERGROUND 1: Underground things

This page can be used as a cover for the topic book, with the title written in the space; or for a poem, for blank verse, or the child's general impressions of the completed topic. Enlarged, it can be used as a class vocabulary sheet, or, kept at A4, as a personal vocabulary sheet.

Vocabulary list

Make a class vocabulary list on a long sheet of paper (the longest list in the whole world!) so the children can build up a bank of words connected with the topic.

Reportive writing

The children can do reportive writing about any trips they have made underground; and they can write from direct observation about any of the scientific activities, e.g. watching the gerbils make their burrow, setting up and recording the 'growing' experiments, building a crane.

UNDERGROUND 2: Simple crossword

This simple puzzle introduces children to the basic rules of crosswords and to some interesting topic words.

Imaginative writing

Discuss what it might be like to be lost in an underground cave system or to be an animal that lives its life mostly underground (this could be a real animal or 'the monster from the pit'!). Or rewrite the Greek legend of *Theseus and the Minotaur*. *Blueprints: Writing* in this series provides many sheets that could be used for imaginative writing in this topic area: the 'special machine' could travel or tunnel underground; the 'secret door' could lead to a maze of underground passages and network of rooms containing . . . the lair of the 'giant caterpillar' or the 'dragon's' cave. All the sheets are suitable for verse or narrative work and, in some cases, will extend illustrative skills. See also *PIRATES 5: Race for the treasure* on page 149 of this book for stimulus for a treasure-hunt story.

UNDERGROUND 3: Underground adventure

Use this picture as a starting point for a story. You can discuss with the children where the cavern leads to, who made the steps, does anyone live in the hole, is there light down there, is it cold or warm, etc. Ask the children to imagine what they might find at the bottom of the steps: a monster, treasure, a lost pet, an injured person, a fantasy world, a time warp . . .

Poems

Read relevant poems and verses, e.g. 'Ding, Dong Bell'; 'Jack and Jill'; and the poignant and descriptive poem about the horrors of a miner's life, *Don't go down the Mine, Dad.*

MATHEMATICS

UNDERGROUND 4: Escape to the surface

This game provides practice in counting-on and recognising numbers up to 50; it can be played by two or more players, but is probably best with just two. The players take turns to throw a dice and move a counter on the correct number of spaces. If a worm (counter) lands on a square where it could be spotted by a mole, it has to stay very still to avoid being seen, so the player misses a go. Make sure the players use counters of different colours. The winner is the first to get to the surface by reaching 50.

Measuring growth

This is a simple experiment using broad beans, glass or plastic jars, blotting-paper and water. Put a little water in a jar and a roll of blotting-paper. Make the roll fairly tight so that the bean, when you slip it down the side, will not fall straight to the bottom. Put the jar in a cool cupboard until the bean germinates, but observe it from day one and record the observations carefully. Drawings are a good method of recording here. The children should be encouraged to be meticulous and accurate in their drawings and measurements.

UNDERGROUND 5: Growth graphs

This sheet is a simple graph which can be used to record either the root or shoot growth of the beans. The vertical axis represents a centimetre ruler, on which the children can write the numbers before possibly colouring it to look like a school ruler. The numbering must go from top to bottom or bottom to top, according to whether you are using the graph for root or shoot growth. The top and bottom horizontal axes should be used for pictures of the bean and numbering the days, as shown.

You can ask the children to draw in the beans and number the days, or you can do it yourself on the first copy and then copy the rest from that one. The children can then colour the beans and add the root/shoot growth, which they should draw daily. If you carry on for more than one week, simply attach another sheet (minus the ruler) at the right-hand side. You can set up as many jars as is practical, maybe one for every six children, and record the growth daily for as long as you feel necessary (don't forget to record the days of non-visible growth before germination actually starts). Roots, when delicate, can be measured with a piece of wool against the side of the jar. Later on, when the shoot and roots are stronger, the bean can be taken out carefully and an important part of the lesson should be care of the growing plants.

Root growth

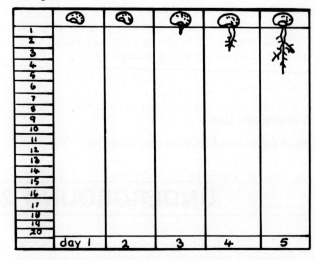

Shoot growth

blotting-paper roll

water

Day 1

Day 2

Day 5

Build a tunnel

Use the sand-tray for this and have water available. Provide various materials like wirenetting (with sharp edges carefully turned in and covered), cardboard tubes, pieces of card or small boxes, and small pieces of wood. The task is to make a tunnel through the sand from one side of the tray to the other and to drive a toy car through it. The roof can be supported or unsupported.

Set up a wormery

See page 65 in the topic section *Homes* for instructions about how to do this. An ant 'town' can also be set up, and these are available from suppliers of scientific materials for schools.

Set up a gerbil tank

Buy or borrow a pair of gerbils (they are happier in pairs and you will get more tunnels). You will need a *large* glass aquarium with a secure net-frame top. Fill this three-quarters full of garden soil, add a few rocks and put turf on top. Keep this well watered. You can add a ball of wool and then stand back to watch the gerbils bury rocks, turn wool into a nest and create a network of tunnels. See the topic section *Pets* for longer-term care of animals in school.

Make a root-top garden

Cut the tops off some root vegetables and set them in a shallow dish of water in a light spot. After a few days you will be able to see roots peeping from the sides of the tops and the foliage will also grow on. This provides a simple example of how plants create a root system to extract goodness from the soil.

Grow a hyacinth in water

This is a deservedly popular activity and, once it has flowered, the bulb can be planted in the garden to die down naturally, ready for next year's growth. Onions will produce an extensive root system under similar conditions, but do not flower so extravagantly. If possible, get hold of an ornamental onion because these are more fun.

Make lifting gear for a well

Use junk or construction-kit materials for this activity. The well-head needs to be quite high so support it on something that will also create the well (e.g. polystyrene packaging). Show the children pictures of a well's winding gear or, if possible, a real well, and then give them the materials. Their task is to make the winding gear and ensure that it can be turned by a handle. A crane can also be made by this method. You can introduce a weight to be lifted to make the problem more taxing for veteran well-builders. You will also need a counter-weight to balance that of the lifting gear.

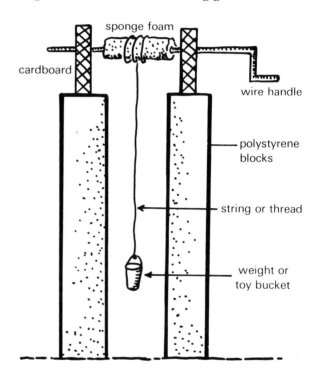

Wax rubbings

Use strong, thick wax crayons to take rubbings of manhole covers, hydrant covers, grills and gratings – anything that covers a means of access underground. Make sure the subjects are clean!

Quilling

Link this to the cylindrical shape of pipes which go underground. Wrap strips of coloured paper round a pencil and display them inside a large circle of paper or a section from a large cardboard tube.

Tube sculpture

Provide the children with cardboard tubes of as many different lengths and widths as possible: these are the pipes. Let the children explore them freely and design their own sculptures. Discuss problems of fixing the tubes together, and try out different glues. Finally decorate the models.

The models need not be abstract. The children may prefer to construct a fantasy castle or an underground tube-city or a moon-rocket.

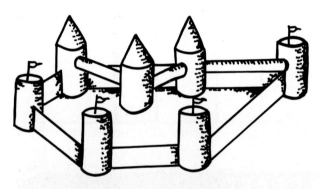

corrugated card

Cut tubes or quills.

Mount on a base.

With various card shapes, corrugated card and some quilling they could produce a fantastic machine, a peculiar robot or a firework display.

Thumb-pots

Take a lump of clay and explore its properties; squash, squeeze, pinch, pull, press, stretch, roll. Make a thumb-pot by taking a ball of clay and pressing the thumb into the centre. The children can add decoration by adding small pieces which have been squashed, squeezed, pinched, pressed or rolled; or different implements can be used to make marks in the clay.

Painting

Use the marbling technique to illustrate the patterns that oil makes on water (see page 54) in the topic section *Water*).

This topic offers numerous subjects for free, expressive painting: trains, barges and underground railways and tunnels; machinery for excavation work; underground rivers; volcanoes and geysers; etc.

For cave interiors, including stalactites and stalagmites, use a multimedia approach. Draw the rock structures first with yellow, brown and white wax crayons and then put a black wash over the top. Add small scraps of Cellophane® and coloured foil to represent precious metals and gemstones.

Early man painted the caves themselves. Use illustrations of the cave-paintings of Lascaux as inspiration and a starting point, and let the children finger-paint and hand-print on rock-coloured activity paper. They could also try to make their own brushes.

Jewellery

To make fake jewellery, stick pasta shapes, acorn cups, nutshells, dried seeds, etc. onto pieces of card and spray them with gold and silver metallic paint (use ozone friendly sprays). Glue safety-pins on the back of brooches. The same technique can be used to make crowns, tiaras and bracelets, with additional 'jewels' of coloured foil or cellophane.

To display your collection of jewellery, decorate a box as a treasure chest.

pasta

acorn cups

macaroni

MUSIC

Listen to *Fingal's Cave* by Mendelssohn and extracts from *Peer Gynt* by Grieg. Try making echoes in rooms, boxes, bottles and cans and sing songs as rounds to achieve an echo-effect. Learn the Wombles' song.

DANCE, DRAMA AND PE

Mime the various actions concerned with underground work: digging, burrowing, a spinning drill, pulling trucks, climbing up and down, pulling, pushing, wriggling like a worm.

Turn the home corner into a cave by covering the top (if any) with a black sheet or old brown curtain. Remove furniture and try to provide synthetic fur-fabric 'animal skins' and some wild animals (stuffed toys) which the children can imagine are mammoths and sabre-toothed tigers.

RELIGIOUS EDUCATION

Talk about dying and the custom of burial in various cultures. Look at some of the monuments to people who have died, and perhaps visit a local church and look at the headstones. It may be possible to get permission to take rubbings of these or of any brasses in the church.

Stories could include the raising of Lazarus (from the New Testament) and, of course, the story of the resurrection of Christ.

ENVIRONMENTAL STUDIES

UNDERGROUND 6: I-spy holes

This pictorial checklist is for use during a walk around the school or neighbourhood. The three empty spaces are for your own additions. Many children do not realise that the items illustrated 'lead' underground in some way.

UNDERGROUND 7: Crossword

The theme of this crossword is the underground homes of various animals. The children should know, or be able to find out, the answers to clues 1 to 6. The mole's tunnels are called a fortress – the children may need your help with that one!

Other lines of research

Find out as much as you can about some of these subjects.

- Underground transport.
- Other underground services: gas, sewage, water, etc.
- The history of mining, with particular reference to child labour in the past.
- Fossils, especially local fossils. Visit a museum or, even better, a local site. Discuss the relationship of fossils to fossil fuels and their formation.

Underground 1

114

Going underground

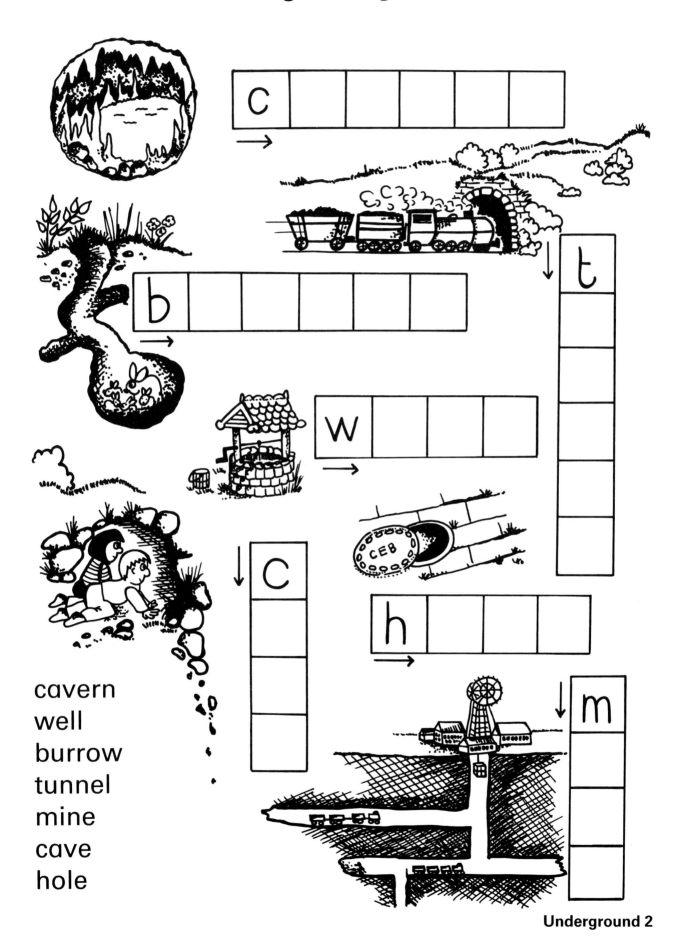

c _ _ _ _ _

b _ _ _ _ _

w _ _ _

t (vertical)

c (vertical)

h _ _ _

m (vertical)

cavern
well
burrow
tunnel
mine
cave
hole

Underground 2

115

Underground adventure

Escape to the surface

Underground 4

117

Growth graph

I spy holes going underground.

Tick a box when you spot one of these holes

plughole	drainpipe	hand-access cover
manhole cover	grating	yellow emergency water supply
downpipe	toilet	exterior cellar doors

Home search

Clues

Across **4** Rabbits dig a huge w _ _ _ _ _ _.
5 A kingfisher's hole is in
a r _ _ _ _ _ _ _ _.
7 A mole's tunnels are called
a f _ _ _ _ _ _ _.

Down **1** A fox sleeps in a l _ _ _.
2 Another name for this is a d _ _.
3 A bat hangs in a c _ _ _.
6 Birds build a n _ _ _ in Spring.

Underground 7

120

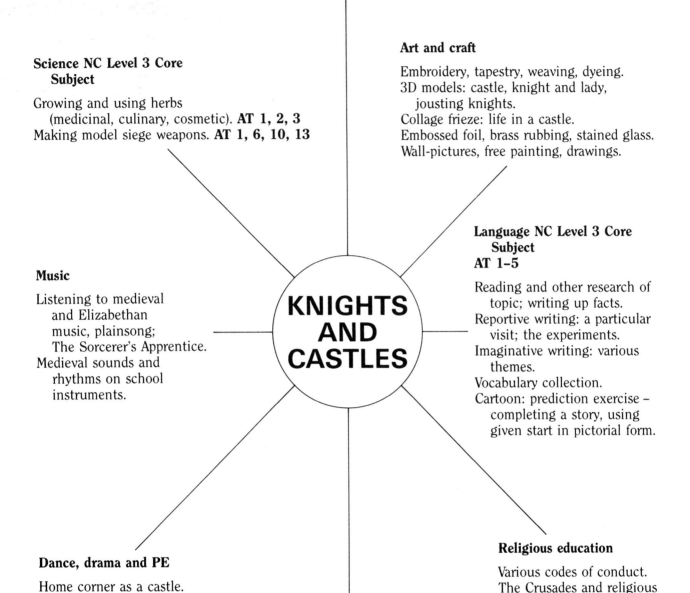

**Mathematics NC Level 3 Core
Subject**

Learning draughts and chess. **AT 1, 9, 11**
Plane and solid shapes (revision). **AT 1, 9, 10, 11**
Game: recognition of numbers up
    to 30; counting on. **AT 1, 2, 9**
Measuring distances in metres. **AT 1, 8, 9**

Art and craft

Embroidery, tapestry, weaving, dyeing.
3D models: castle, knight and lady,
    jousting knights.
Collage frieze: life in a castle.
Embossed foil, brass rubbing, stained glass.
Wall-pictures, free painting, drawings.

**Science NC Level 3 Core
Subject**

Growing and using herbs
    (medicinal, culinary, cosmetic). **AT 1, 2, 3**
Making model siege weapons. **AT 1, 6, 10, 13**

**Language NC Level 3 Core
Subject
AT 1–5**

Reading and other research of
    topic; writing up facts.
Reportive writing: a particular
    visit; the experiments.
Imaginative writing: various
    themes.
Vocabulary collection.
Cartoon: prediction exercise –
    completing a story, using
    given start in pictorial form.

Music

Listening to medieval
    and Elizabethan
    music, plainsong;
    The Sorcerer's Apprentice.
Medieval sounds and
    rhythms on school
    instruments.

KNIGHTS AND CASTLES

Religious education

Various codes of conduct.
The Crusades and religious
    attitudes today.
Medieval customs and
    traditions.

Dance, drama and PE

Home corner as a castle.
Mime: banquet, joust.
Dances and processions.

Environmental studies

Locations of castles in Britain.
Details of the interior of a keep.
Visit to a castle.

KNIGHTS AND CASTLES

BASIC CONCEPTS

1 Castles were built for people to live in safely and to stop invasion.

2 The best place to build a castle for safety and defence was on high ground surrounded by water.

3 Most castles were built for knights, barons or monarchs.

4 Knights, lords and barons were people who helped the monarch. In return they were given lands which they defended with strong castles.

5 Each knight had his own flag with special patterns on it, so that he could be recognised. This developed into heraldry.

6 Many people lived and worked in a castle.

7 Life in a castle was very different from our lives today.

STARTING POINT

If possible, visit a castle. There are many castles which cater for school parties, and the Regional Tourist Board will have details. Cadw (Welsh historical monuments) is responsible for many Welsh castles, and information can also be obtained from The National Trust for England, Wales and Northern Ireland; the Scottish National Trust; and English Heritage. Photographs and a wallchart of medieval castles is available from the Pictorial Charts Educational Trust.

Compile a selection of clips from videos, or watch videos such as *Robin Hood, Hawk the Slayer, Richard the Lionheart, The Sword in the Stone* and *The Vikings*. A video called *The Castle* is available from Viewtech Audio-visual Media, 161 Winchester Road, Brislington, Bristol BS4 3NJ.

The children could bring in toy castles and knights; you could also make a collection of books about castles, clothes, costume, armour, customs, weapons, heraldry and chivalry. If possible try to visit a castle that has displays of jousting and falconry. Gwrych Castle in North Wales has jousting and Sudely Castle in Winchcombe, Gloucester has falconry. Some castles have historical 'experiences' for which the children dress in the clothes of the period and spend the day doing activities to match.

Because so many different types of castle have been built and used over a period of several centuries, the best approach to the topic might be to concentrate on one particular castle and take all examples of castle life from the period of its heyday. A comparison of different styles of castle could be made with the chosen one.

Besides using the reference and topic books, read fiction and fairy stories like *Rapunzel, The Sleeping Beauty, King Arthur and the Knights of the Round Table,* and *St George and the Dragon.*

LANGUAGE

After the children have had their interest aroused through stories, poems, books and pictures, videos and visits, encourage them to write up the facts they have discovered about knights and castles. They could also do reportive writing about any visits and about the experiments suggested later on in this section.

KNIGHTS AND CASTLES 1: Coversheet

This is a dual-purpose sheet which can be used as a cover for the topic book or as two separate pages for imaginative writing. To use one half, simply cover the unwanted one with a sheet of blank paper before photocopying. One half shows a composite of historic people and the other shows castles through the ages. Discuss feudal life and times and then let the children each pretend to be a person who might have lived in a castle, e.g. a knight, a lady, a servant, the steward, a serf, an entertainer, the cook. They can write about their feelings and what they do. Other writing could be about dragons (make up an adventure about the castle being attacked by a giant dragon) or magic and sorcery, which was an important aspect of life and belief in medieval times. Possible themes are Merlin the Magician or a book of old spells found in a ruined castle. Castles often have secret passages and this opens up lots of ideas for an adventure in a ruined castle or a journey through the secret passages by a lost page-boy. What does he find?

Long ago, many people believed in mythical beasts such as the unicorn, the griffin and the winged horse. Use *TRANSPORT 3: Pegasus* (see page 101 of this book) for imaginative writing about magic creatures. Also, *Blueprints: Writing* in this series provides topic sheets concerning spells, Hallowe'en and a dragon.

Prediction exercise

Devise a cartoon strip with six boxes, the first three with pictures ready drawn and the last three empty. The object of the exercise is for children, individually or in pairs, to discuss the content of the empty boxes in the light of the information given in the first three boxes, and make up an ending for the cartoon. The first three boxes could contain a damsel in distress, a dragon, and a knight on horseback. Suggestions for the remaining three are the knight fighting the dragon, the dragon dead and the knight freeing the damsel, and the knight and maiden returning home to grateful castle folk. However the children may wish to have an unhappy ending or a friendly dragon.

MATHEMATICS

Teach the children to play chess and draughts, both of which were popular games in the medieval period. Both games involve strategy, and chess, of course, uses terms such as castle, knight and bishop. Try to get hold of one of the medieval chess sets which are now mass-produced and have little figures which you could also use on a display or in the toy castle. Revise the terms *vertical,* *horizontal* and *diagonal*, these being the various moves the pieces can make.

Revise plane and solid shapes and look for examples of cones, cylinders, cuboids and triangular prisms in castle architecture. This will be useful preparation for building a model castle (see the section on *Art and craft*).

KNIGHTS AND CASTLES 2: Shields

This sheet shows a large outline shield and two strips of small shields partitioned in various ways with line designs. The children can colour all of these, using the large shield to design a coat of arms for themselves or their family.

Discuss symmetry. Some children like 'balanced' patterns and they may notice that many medieval patterns are symmetrical.

The large shields can be cut out and used as part of a display; and the strips could form part of a diorama. Also, if you blank out the central shield when photocopying, you can run off as many sheets as you like with just the strips as borders. These can be used for the topic book and for any writing or drawing; the coloured borders will create the effect of an illuminated manuscript, so typical of the period.

KNIGHTS AND CASTLES 3: Storm the keep!

This game is on two sheets which should be Sellotaped together. The game, which is for two or more players, practises counting on and recognition of numbers up to thirty. Players take turns to throw a dice and move a counter on according to the number thrown (players' counters should be of different colours). Players start at number one on the outer ring and have to keep going round until they land on one of the gaps in the defences (the tinted sections). Then they can move into the next ring at the adjacent number. The same rule applies for this ring, and so players reach the third circle. The object of the game is to reach the door of the keep before any other player, but this must be done with an *exact throw*. A player can choose not to move if his/her throw will take the counter past the drawbridge; once on the drawbridge (tinted sections 1, 2 and 3) a throw of 2 or 1 is required.

Suppose, for example, a player in this position throws a 6.

He or she cannot reach the door and would go past the drawbridge, but can choose to stop at 9. Now suppose the player throws a 3 instead of a 6. The counter can be moved to number 2, leaving the child requiring a 1. A throw of 4 instead of 3 would be a winning throw.

Measuring

Using trundle-wheels, children could take measurements during a visit to a castle, and then draw these out on the playground or sports field, to get a better idea of comparative size away from the site itself.

Also, you could tell the children that archers with longbows were able to shoot arrows up to a distance of 180 metres. The children could then measure out that distance using a trundle-wheel. Do it in stages: 5 m, 10 m, 15 m, . . . 180 m.

SCIENCE

Growing and using herbs

Most castles had a herb garden. Find out about the uses of herbs for medicinal, culinary and cosmetic purposes. The children would enjoy growing their own herbs, either in pots or in the school garden if there is one. There are many herbals available which give instructions on how to make rose-petal water, lavender water, mint sauce, lavender pouches, etc. We use many of the herbs today for the same purpose.

Siege weapons

Look at the diagrams or models of the siege weapons of the day and get the children to make working models of such things as the battering ram, the portcullis and the drawbridge. Provide junk materials, assorted glues, balsa wood, pins, paper-clips and tools, and allow the children to experiment, ask questions and discuss the problems of construction between themselves and with you.

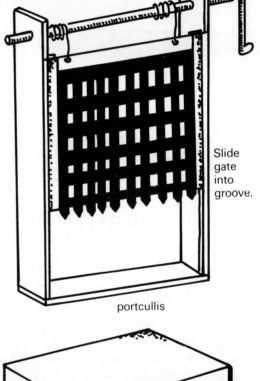

Slide gate into groove.

portcullis

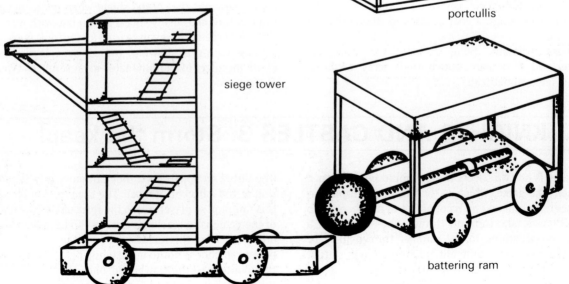

siege tower

battering ram

A model castle

'Build' a model castle with cartons, tubes, card and paper. Litre fruit-juice or milk cartons, well washed, will make square towers, and half-litre cartons will make the tops of towers or castle buildings. For round towers, use plastic squeezy bottles with the tops removed or concealed.

Tapestry and embroidery

Use Binca® to make a sampler of stitches and for simple tapestry work with wools. Chevrons and stripes are fairly easy designs to start with, and the finished piece of tapestry can be made into a pouch such as a medieval person might have worn to keep money in.

Try weaving and dyeing natural materials (see pages 82 and 83 in the topic section *Clothes*).

Collage

Use pieces of material to make a large collage of castle life, and hang this on the wall. The material will invest the collage with a tapestry 'feel' and you can use it to demonstrate how tapestries which 'told stories' were hung on the walls of castles. Show the children pictures of the Bayeux tapestry.

Models of a knight and his lady

The base for each model is a cardboard tube covered with crepe paper or material. The arms are one long paper strip glued round the back of the tube.

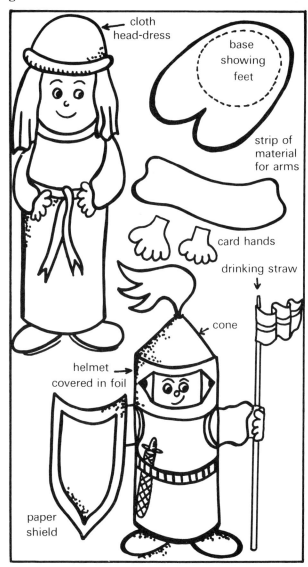

KNIGHTS AND CASTLES 4: Knights on horseback

Colour the two sides of the figure, cut them out and fix them together as shown. Explain to the children how this is done *before* they start colouring, so that they realise the sheet makes *one* two-sided model. The figures can be used for a jousting diorama.

Embossed patterns

The idea of these patterns is to simulate embossed metalwork on armour. First you will need to make patterns using thick string glued onto stiff card. Cover the whole of the pattern with PVA glue.

Take a piece of aluminium foil about twice the size of the card, and press this very carefully onto the glued surface so that the raised string pattern shows through but does not tear the foil. Leave to dry, and then you can emphasise the pattern by rubbing black shoe polish into it and wiping off the surplus.

Brass rubbings and stained glass

If possible, go to a brass-rubbing centre or make arrangements to do rubbings at a local church. Often brasses show good examples of the costume, armour and heraldry of the period. The technique for making 'stained-glass windows' is described on page 68.

Pictures

The children can design their own large wall-picture of a castle, using the knowledge they have gained about defences and lifestyles, and a multi-media approach, i.e. crayons, felt-tip pens, chalk, collage and paint altogether in the one picture. Another subject for a large painting or collage is St George and the dragon.

Themes for free painting could include witches, magic, feasts, markets, washing the clothes, cooking; and it would be worth while letting the children draw pieces of armour, weapons and possibly furniture, either from direct observation or using book references.

MUSIC

Listen to medieval music if possible (Elizabethan music has a similar quality) and to examples of plainsong from early church music. Try to find pictures of medieval instruments and, using the school instruments like tabour, drum and recorder, you could try to reproduce some of the rhythms and sounds of the period. To link with the themes of magic and witchcraft listen to *The Sorcerer's Apprentice* by Paul Dukas.

Turn the home corner into a castle with crenellations on the top and, possibly, towers of corrugated cardboard at each corner. Inside, include two thrones for a knight and his lady, and provide costumes such as cloaks, coronets, tabards, armour, and a hobby-horse for

imaginative play. Children can each pretend to be one of the people who lived in a castle and this may lead to short scenes of daily life.

Use medieval music in PE and dance sessions and let the children mime the actions of jesters and jugglers and travelling groups of entertainers. Movement vocabulary should include *tumbling, rolling, leaping, bowing* and *balancing*. Process in state round the hall in a slow dignified manner. Contrast these courtly movements with the more abandoned movements of the tumblers and jesters and the villagers dancing round the maypole. Let the children pretend they are lords and ladies dancing, or mime a banquet or a joust.

RELIGIOUS EDUCATION

Talk about the knights' code of conduct and what is meant by chivalry. Link this with school rules, the law of the land, rules of etiquette and general good behaviour. Look at the rules of Brownies and Cubs.

Talk about the Crusades and the differences between the cultures involved. Find out about Muslims today, and help the children to realise that by learning about different peoples and religions we can gain a greater

understanding of each other and have a better chance of living in peace together.

Find out about some of the festivals, customs and traditions of the medieval period, especially those which still survive today. These include May Day celebrations, some Easter and Christmas customs (the Lord of Misrule), All Hallows Eve.

KNIGHTS AND CASTLES 5: People from around 1500

This information sheet can be used as it is, or each side can be reproduced on an A4 sheet, leaving space for extra information or drawings. The figures can be coloured, copied or cut out, in which case they can be included in a diorama as standing models. It is best to keep them at A5 size for use as models. Have reference books available so that the children can colour the figures authentically if they wish.

Castles of Britain

Draw an outline map of the British Isles or use a mapograph roller, and photocopy this for each child in your class. Teacher and children together decide which castles to show: local or national, border or coastal, etc. Show your own home town and the major cities of today so that the children gradually learn their locations. Use a simple symbol to show the sites of castles.

KNIGHTS AND CASTLES 6: Inside a keep

This shows the major parts of the building. Using the topic books, the children can put in details of the interiors from dungeon to battlements.

KNIGHTS AND CASTLES 7: Castle buildings

This sheet shows various castle structures, labelled with the correct vocabulary. At the bottom of the sheet there is a simple cloze procedure for the children to complete. The children could try to build a model of one of the earliest forts – a motte and bailey – using the sand-tray, twigs for the fencing, and small boxes for the buildings.

950–1200

1086–1200

1275–1300

1300–1500

Knights and castles 1

Knights and castles 2

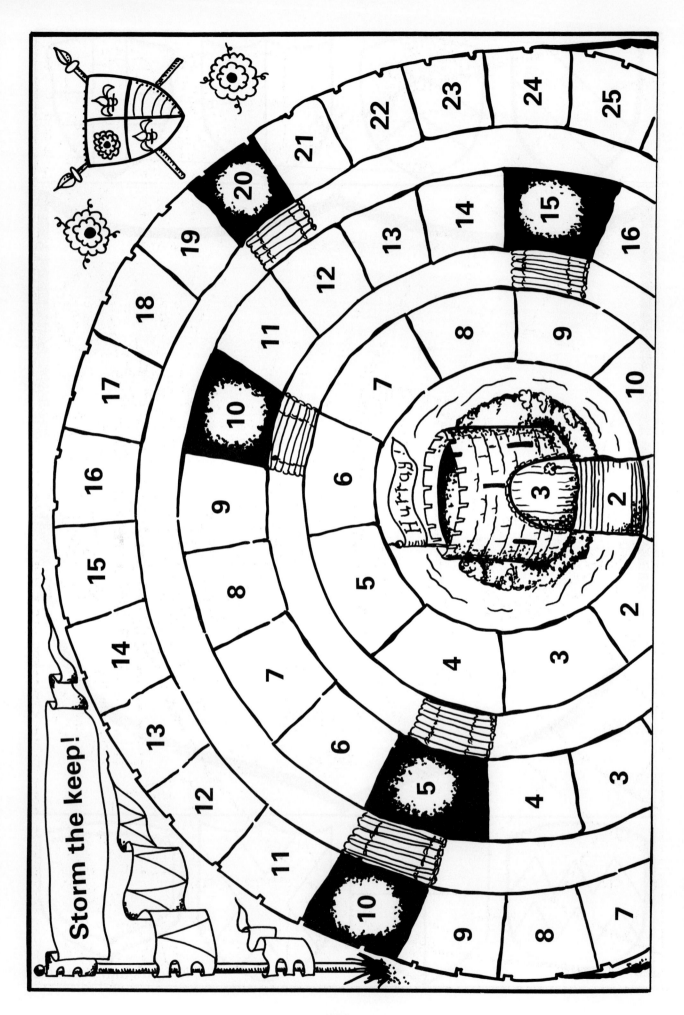

Storm the keep!

130

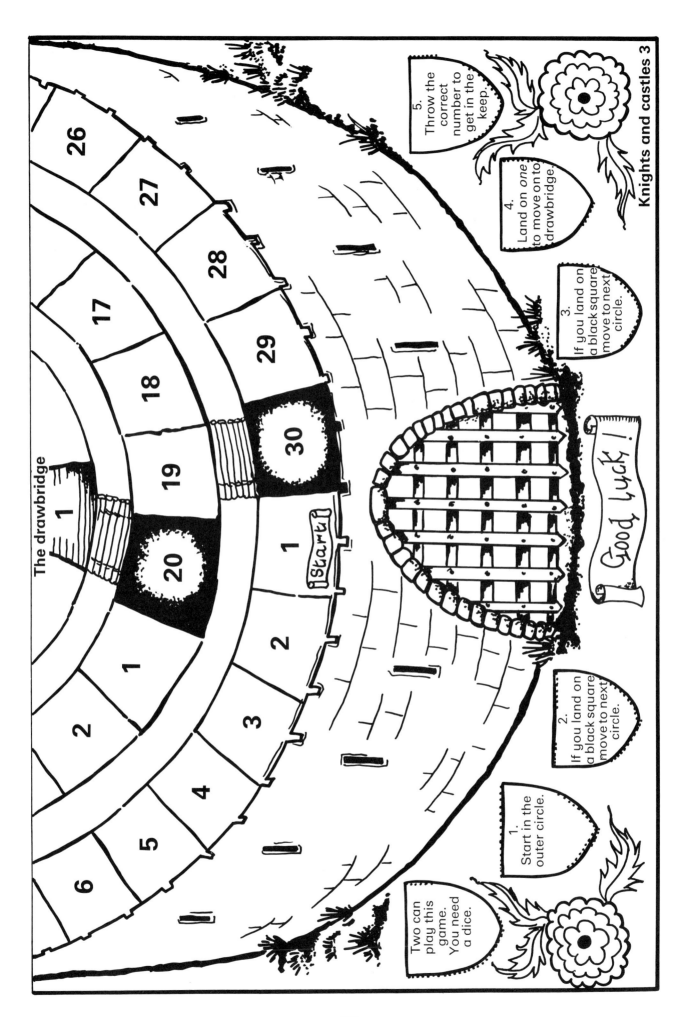

The drawbridge

26
27
28
29
30
17
18
19
20
1
1
2
1
2
3
4
5
6

¡Start!

Good luck!

1.
Start in the
outer circle.

2.
If you land on
a black square
move to next
circle.

3.
If you land on
a black square
move to next
circle.

4.
Land on *one*
to move onto
drawbridge.

5.
Throw the
correct
number to
get in the
keep.

Two can
play this
game.
You need
a dice.

cut

cut

Knights and castles 4

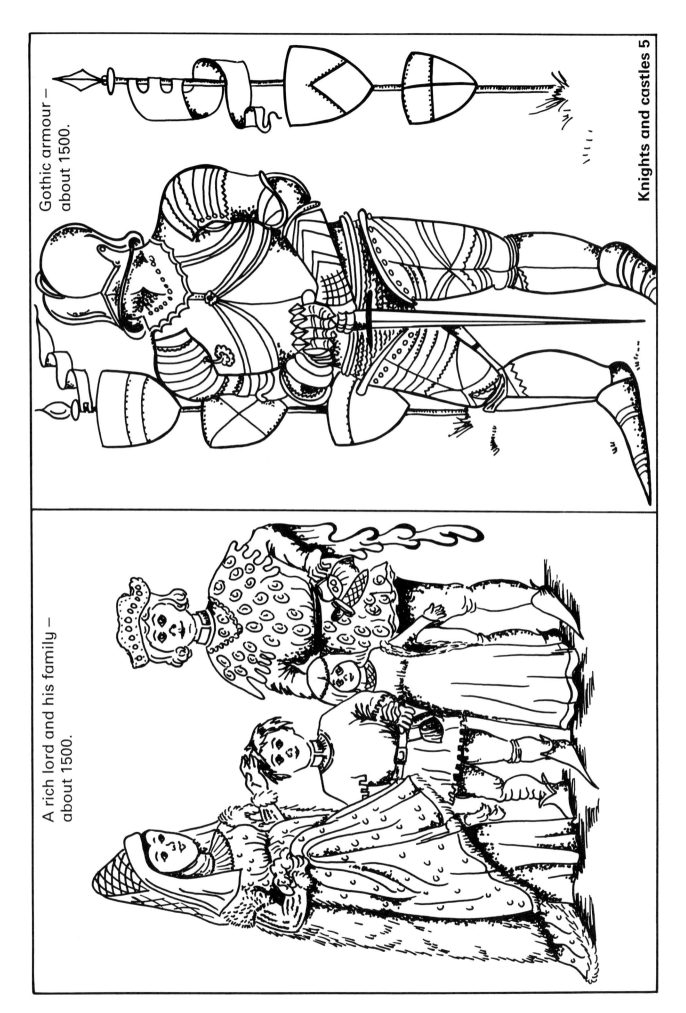

Gothic armour – about 1500.

A rich lord and his family – about 1500.

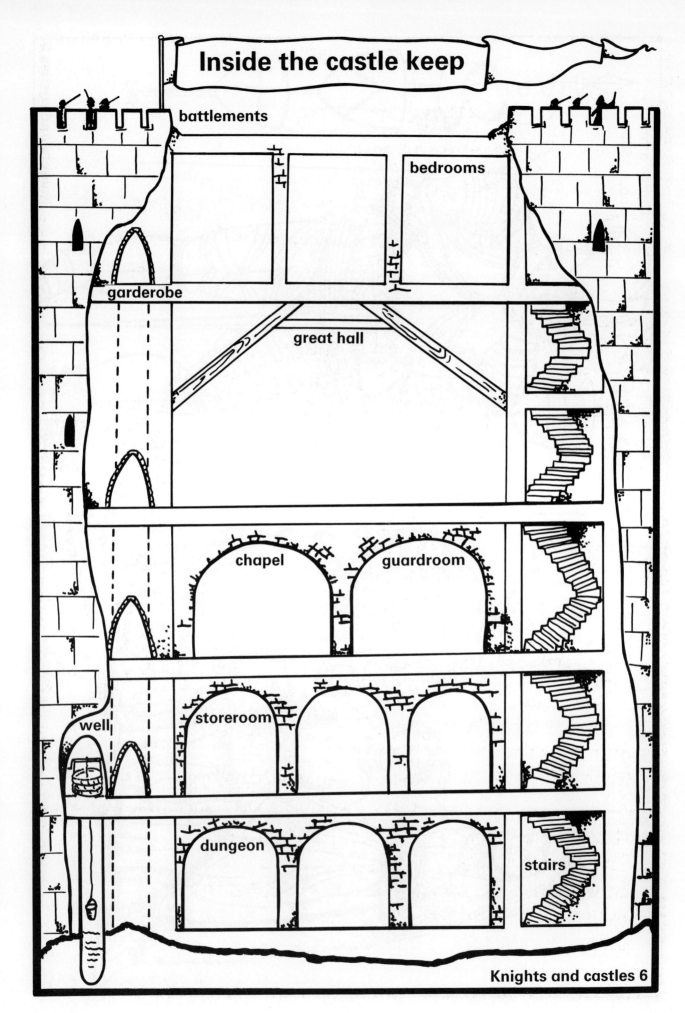

Inside the castle keep

battlements

bedrooms

garderobe

great hall

chapel

guardroom

well

storeroom

dungeon

stairs

Knights and castles 6

134

Castle buildings

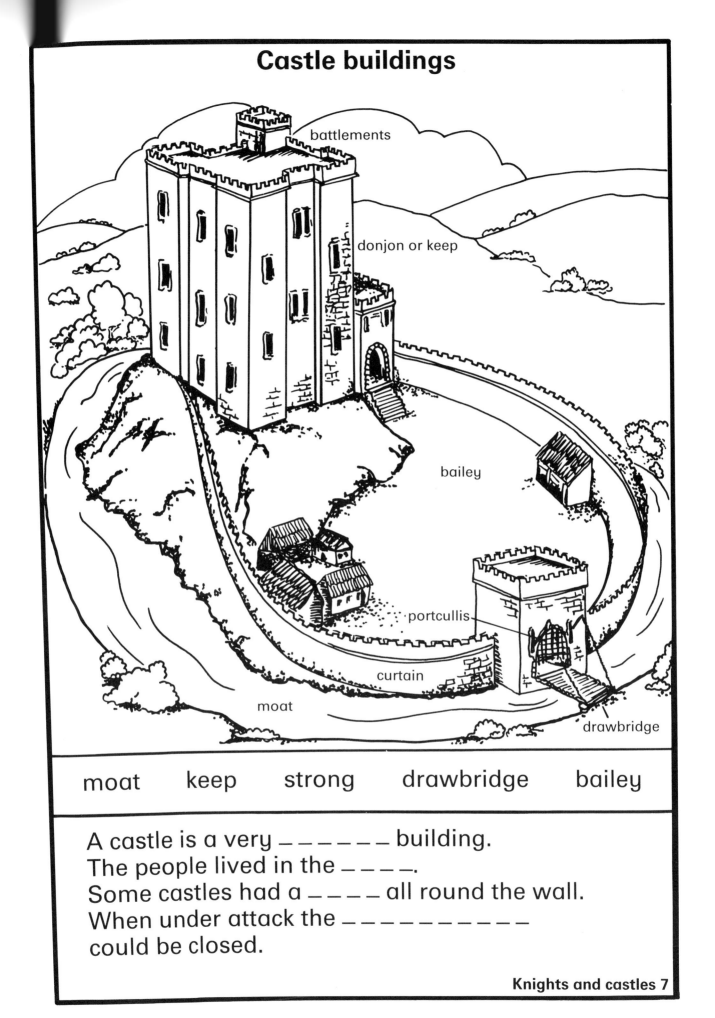

moat   keep   strong   drawbridge   bailey

A castle is a very _ _ _ _ _ _ building.
The people lived in the _ _ _ _.
Some castles had a _ _ _ _ all round the wall.
When under attack the _ _ _ _ _ _ _ _ _ _
could be closed.

Knights and castles 7

135

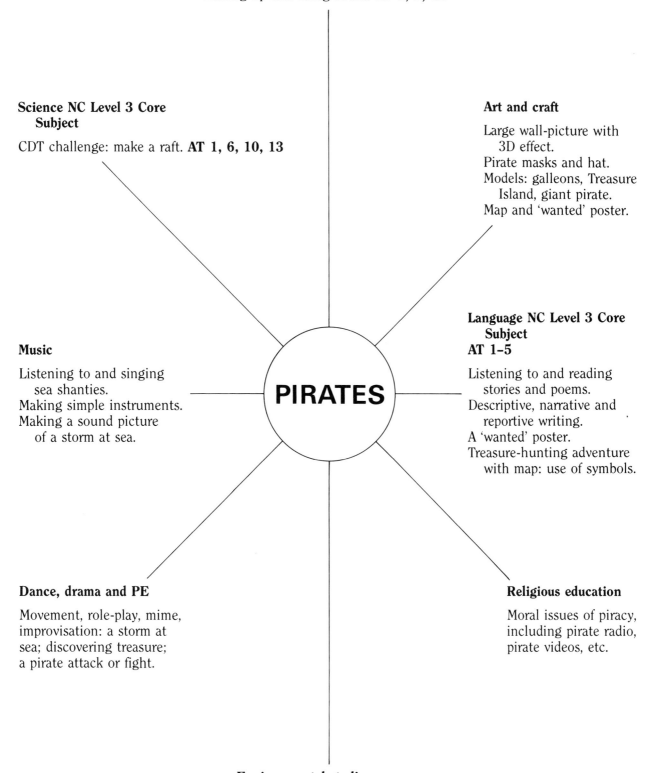

**Mathematics NC Level 3 Core
Subject**

Counting-on game. **AT 1, 2, 9**
Co-ordinates game. **AT 1, 9, 11**
Making up and using codes. **AT 1, 9, 12**

**Science NC Level 3 Core
Subject**

CDT challenge: make a raft. **AT 1, 6, 10, 13**

Art and craft

Large wall-picture with
3D effect.
Pirate masks and hat.
Models: galleons, Treasure
Island, giant pirate.
Map and 'wanted' poster.

Music

Listening to and singing
sea shanties.
Making simple instruments.
Making a sound picture
of a storm at sea.

PIRATES

**Language NC Level 3 Core
Subject
AT 1–5**

Listening to and reading
stories and poems.
Descriptive, narrative and
reportive writing.
A 'wanted' poster.
Treasure-hunting adventure
with map: use of symbols.

Dance, drama and PE

Movement, role-play, mime,
improvisation: a storm at
sea; discovering treasure;
a pirate attack or fight.

Religious education

Moral issues of piracy,
including pirate radio,
pirate videos, etc.

Environmental studies

Visits: museums, historic ships.
Life at sea in past times.
History of piracy.
Geography of the oceans and
areas of frequent piracy.

PIRATES

BASIC CONCEPTS

1 Pirates were sailors who lived and worked on board ship for long periods (years and months).

2 They lived very hard lives.

3 They were mostly men, but there were some women.

4 They were outlaws who made a living by stealing from the people on other ships.

5 There have been pirates at different times in the past, and in different parts of the world.

6 The symbol of a pirate ship was the 'skull and crossbones' flag.

STARTING POINT

Watch the video of Walt Disney's version of Robert Louis Stevenson's *Treasure Island*. Build up a collection of books about pirates and read pirate poems and stories. The *Griffin Readers* by Shelagh McCullagh is one series that features pirate stories: the tales about Roderick the Red Pirate, Benjamin the Blue Pirate and Gregory the Green Pirate are suitable for children of different reading ages.

Children can dress up as pirates for an afternoon, and this will enhance a class discussion about life on board a pirate ship. Talk about the jobs of the various crew members: captain, bo'sun, cabin boy, cook. Talk about the life style: the food (not much fresh food, but salted beef and hardtack), sleeping in hammocks, attacking other ships, plundering, storms at sea, desert islands, treasure, and so on.

LANGUAGE

The starting-point discussion can lead on to writing and blank verse. Themes for this could include *The sea in all its moods, The weather, Hunting for lost treasure, Look-out from the crow's nest, The secret island, The ghostly pirate ship, Shipwrecked, Smuggling*.

Children could write a newspaper account of a pirate attack, a shipwreck or the daring exploits of a famous pirate. Their own drawings of the pirate attack could make covers for their topic books, or for short stories. The

stories of famous pirates can be based on facts known about real-life pirates in history, such as Blackbeard (Edward Teach), Captain Kidd and Long Ben Avery. These stories, together with factual writing about life on board ship, can be individually mounted for class display or gathered into a book for the children to read. The pirate mask (sheet 6 on page 150) could be used as a cover for the book.

PIRATES 1: 'Wanted' poster

Children can invent their own pirates by making 'wanted' posters each consisting of a descriptive passage underneath a picture. Tell them not to forget to invent a terrible deed of piracy as well.

PIRATES 2: Treasure Island

This is a basic outline map of a secret island. The children can complete the map and mark where the treasure is buried. Show them how to use symbols like those shown here to represent features, and how to finish the key.

The children could write about how they explored their island, faced its dangers and, perhaps, found the treasure.

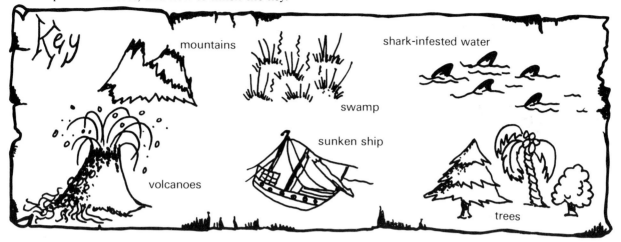

MATHEMATICS

PIRATES 3: Pirate battle

This simple game of co-ordinates is played by two children, each of whom has a copy of the sheet. The children colour and cut out the small galleons and stick them on their sheets wherever they like. It is very important that neither child sees the opponent's sheet because that would ruin the game.

One child calls out a pair of co-ordinates, e.g. 5 squares up and 4 squares across. The listener finds the appropriate square on his or her own sheet and marks it with a red cross. If the cross lands on a galleon it counts as a 'hit' and the galleon is sunk. Then the children swap roles and the listener becomes the caller. In order to remember which squares he or she has tried, the caller can put a small pencil mark in each square called. The game continues like this, with the players taking turns to call, until one of them sinks his/her opponent's fleet of galleons and wins the game.

PIRATES 4: Secret codes

Many pirate maps were written using secret codes; the sheet contains some simple ones to use with the children.

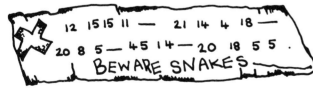

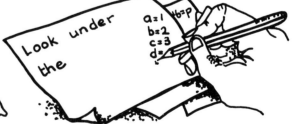

PIRATES 5: Race for the treasure

This game, which is played by two children according to the standard rules, practises counting on. Make sure the counters are of different colours to avoid confusion.

Introduce variations if you want to, e.g. having to throw a six to start; sending your opponent's counter back to the start, if you land on top of it.

SCIENCE

CDT challenge: make a raft

Set the children the task of making a model of a raft to escape from a desert island. Collect a wide range of objects which the children will need to test for floating and sinking. They will then have to decide how to join these items together to make a raft. You will need to supply a range of 'joining' things, e.g. strings, elastic bands, glues and adhesive tapes.

For older children extend the challenge by asking them to design a raft which will carry a figure, e.g. an Action Man® dressed as a pirate. The design of the raft will then have to be tailored to the weight and size of the figure.

Encourage the making of drawings and plans before and after construction. The addition of a sail and a keel increases the range of variables. The children could test for the most effective shape of sail, e.g. triangle, square, rectangle; and whether a keel helps stability in wind or rough seas. Discuss with the children how to simulate wind and wave action.

ART AND CRAFT

This topic lends itself to a really colourful class display. Some suggestions follow.

PIRATES 6: Pirate mask

The children can colour this picture with crayons or paint. Then it can be cut out and stuck onto card for use as a mask, or used as part of your wall display. The coloured sheet also makes an effective book cover. Note that you may need to enlarge the mask by about 25 per cent when photocopying.

3D mask

You can make a mask with a three-dimensional effect by cutting shapes out of activity paper and assembling them. You will need these component pieces:

- the basic face shape (1) and nose (2) cut from paper of the same colour;
- a knotted scarf shape (3) which can be decorated with crayons or paint;
- two pieces of hair (4) – black activity paper, fringed;
- a black patch (5);
- a large black moustache (6)
- a black beard (7) – activity paper fringed and curled with scissors.

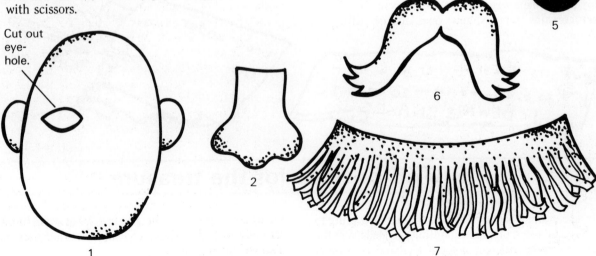

3 with 4 in position

4

5

6

1

2

7

Cut out eye-hole.

To assemble the mask, first add the two pieces of hair and scarf to the basic face shape. Cut out one eye-hole at the level of the ears; then stick on the black patch and the nose. The nose is attached at the top only, which allows it to stick out from the face. Cut a slit for the mouth and then attach the beard and moustache. As a final touch, add two large gold ear-rings made from gold foil.

Pirate hat

Cut two hat shapes from coloured activity paper. Decorate one shape with a skull and crossbones in white paint. Staple or glue together the bottom outer edges, to fit the child's head.

PIRATES 7: Galleon

This sheet provides you with a 3D model of one galleon. Colour each side of the ship, using the same colours for each, and then cut them out carefully. Glue or staple the shapes together around all the edges *except the base*. Insert a circlet of card or a matchbox between the two shapes, to make a flat base as shown. Lightly glue this in place, and you will be able to stand your model in a diorama or model of Treasure Island.

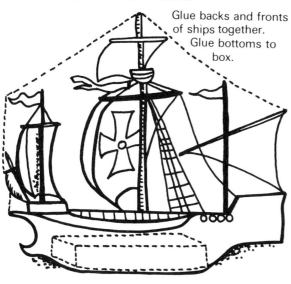

Glue backs and fronts of ships together.
Glue bottoms to box.

Make a Treasure Island

For this you will need to have ready some papier mâché – newspaper torn into small pieces and mixed with wallpaper paste. You will also require a base-board of thick card; sand, glue, twigs, small stones and pebbles, green sponge or tissue paper; green, blue, brown and white paint; PVA glue or varnish; model galleons.

Draw the outline of the island on the base-board, pile on the papier mâché and mould it into an island. Push in twigs to represent trees and position the stones and pebbles as rocks. Wait for the island to dry and then paint in areas of rock in greys and browns, areas of vegetation in greens and the sea in blues and greens. Add waves on the shore by painting crests in lines of white paint. When this is dry, add leaves to the trees by gluing on small pieces of green sponge or tissue paper. Paint the edges of the shore with glue and sprinkle with sand to make beaches. Finally put the paper galleons on the sea.

If you want to incorporate treasure, find a tiny box with a lid, paint it brown and fill with as many small items of treasure as possible, e.g. small beads, ear-rings, charms. Fill one if your papier mâché valleys with sand and bury the treasure in this. If the children are allowed to play carefully with the island, they will sail the ships and discover the treasure daily.

corrugated card background

Main classroom display

A large picture on the most prominent wall of the classroom would provide a focus for the topic work. For this you will need an assortment of coloured activity papers, paints, glue and a stapler. If you make the picture from separate component parts you can achieve a 3D effect.

The central figure of the pirate can be drawn by you; or can be a child's body-shape cut out and painted or assembled from collage shapes by the children. Paint the background of sea, sky and sand on the large backdrop sheet and leave this flat on the floor to dry. Then, separately, paint a palm tree. Some palm leaves can be cut from dark green activity paper and stuck onto the tree to provide the 3D effect.

The spiky grass shapes can be cut from bright green and yellow activity paper.

To assemble the picture, first of all put up the backdrop and then position the palm tree. Stick the tree on, making sure that you bend the leaves outwards slightly before stapling at the top. Staple on the grass, again bending it slightly and overlapping to give the impression of dense growth. Finally position the pirate. Staple one side

142

first then bend the body slightly along the vertical and staple the other side, so that the centre of the body stands out from the wall to give a 3D effect.

To outline the picture, put a border of shaped crepe paper all round the edge or a fringe of skull and crossbone flags.

Make a giant pirate

You will need two or three large cardboard boxes to tape together on top of one another; paint, glue, and black and coloured activity paper.

Paint the body in any colour, possibly red, and the face in flesh tone. Make a hat from black activity paper, large enough to go over the head, and decorate this with a skull and crossbones in white paint. Cut strips of black activity paper into fringes of tooth shapes and stick overlapping layers of these to the head, to form the hair and beard. Decorate the face with a cut-out patch, moustache and painted features. Make two arms from rolls of coloured activity paper. Glue and staple these in position and add two hand shapes. Finally, give the pirate a paper belt and cutlass.

MUSIC

Listen to and learn some sea shanties. Try to sing 'Fifteen Men on a Dead Man's Chest'. Look at some of the instruments the sailors might have played, e.g. the accordian and the penny whistle.

Use untuned percussion instruments to create the sounds of a storm at sea. The children can make some of the instruments themselves:

- shakers of different sorts, e.g. a long cardboard tube containing rice, for the sound of waves on the shore;
- metal waste bins for crashes of thunder;
- large sheets of card for the sounds of the wind.

Talk about the sounds of rain, wind and sea and about what a sailing ship might sound like – creaking timbers, flapping sails, shouting men.

After experimenting with various instruments, try to build up a sound picture. For instance, the storm might start softly, build to a crescendo and then subside to lapping waves and creaking timbers, and finally silence.

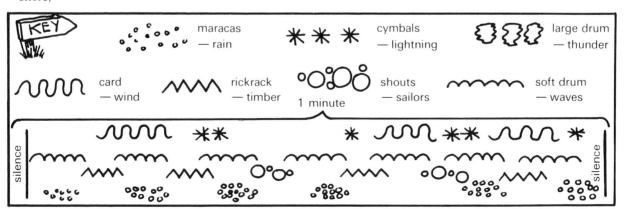

143

DANCE, DRAMA AND PE

Movement lessons can be developed over the weeks of the topic to coincide with the music theme of a storm at sea. Children can be the wind and the waves and move in time to the rhythm of the musical instruments. Pulling, pushing and climbing movements can be linked to the pulling up of the anchor, the pushing round of the capstan, and climbing the rigging. The children can bend, twist and turn for the movements of the sea. The roaring and rushing of the winds and the stillness of a calm sea are strong contrasts, open to many different interpretations.

Mime the digging up of a treasure chest, carrying the chest away and opening it up to reveal . . . what? You could, perhaps, improvise a scene of a pirate crew planning an attack or falling out over the sharing of the gold.

RELIGIOUS EDUCATION

Hold a class discussion about the moral issues of piracy. Examine modern piracy and the use of the word to describe illegal copying – pirate videos and records. What do the children know about pirate radio? Talk about theft in all its forms.

ENVIRONMENTAL STUDIES

Arrange a visit to a maritime museum or to an historic ship such as the *Victory, The Mary Rose* or the *Great Britain*. This will give children some insight into life on board ship and some experience of the artefacts and materials of the time.

Explore books and museums for evidence of pirates through the ages, e.g. the Vikings, the Chinese. Use atlases, globes and maps to look at the position of the world's oceans and the countries frequented by pirates.

Wanted

Dead or alive £500 Reward

Pirates 1

145

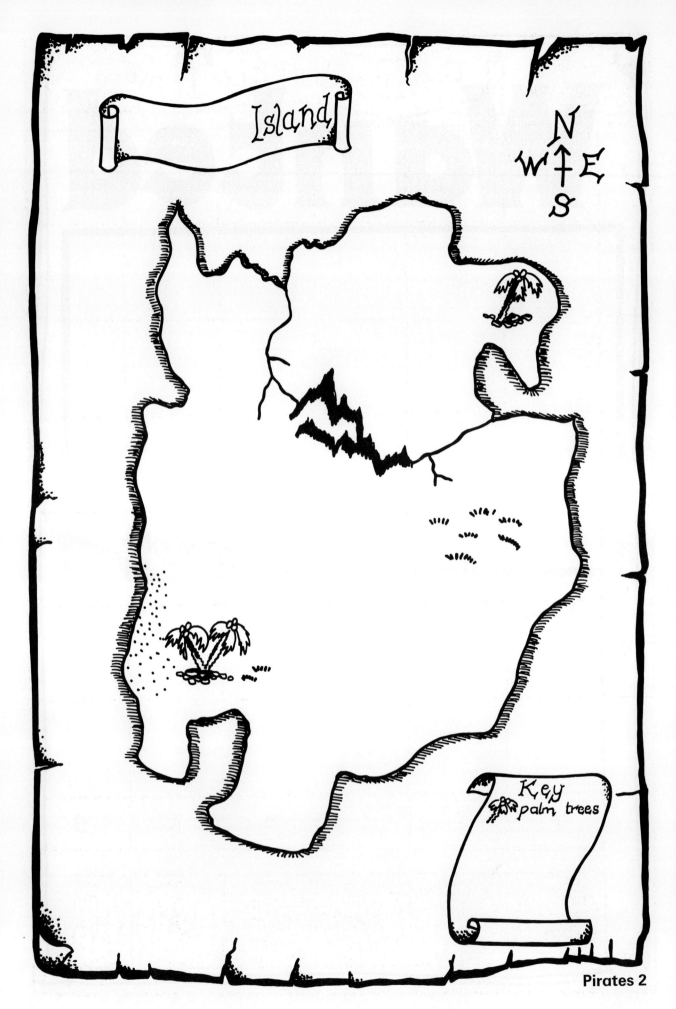

Island

N
W E
S

Key
palm trees

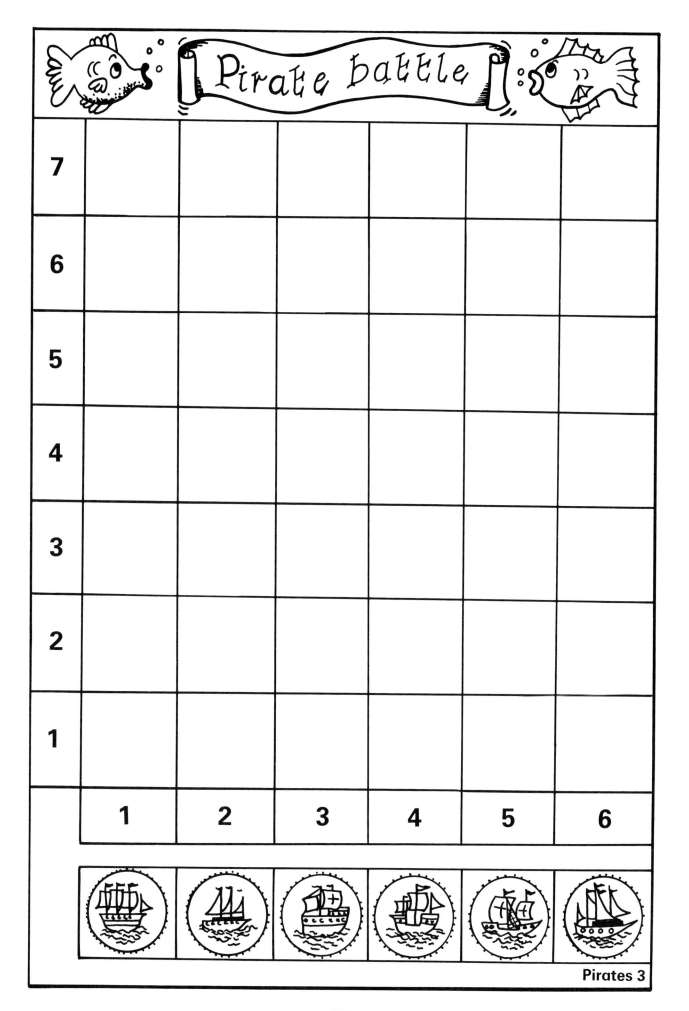

Pirate battle

	1	2	3	4	5	6
7						
6						
5						
4						
3						
2						
1						

Pirates 3

Secret codes

This is a name written in code.

6 18 5 4 4 9 5   6 9 19 8

Here is the code.

a	b	c	d	e	f	g	h	i	j	k	l	m
1	2	3	4	5	6	7	8	9	10	11	12	13

n	o	p	q	r	s	t	u	v	w	x	y	z
14	15	16	17	18	19	20	21	22	23	24	25	26

Work out the name and write it here.

Now write your **own** name in code here.

Messages can be written backwards, like this.

ehT erusaert si deirub ni eht evac.

Turn each word round to read the message.

Write it here.

Write your **own** name in this code.

Make up your own code using a sign for each letter.

a =   b =   c =   and so on.   **Pirates 4**

148

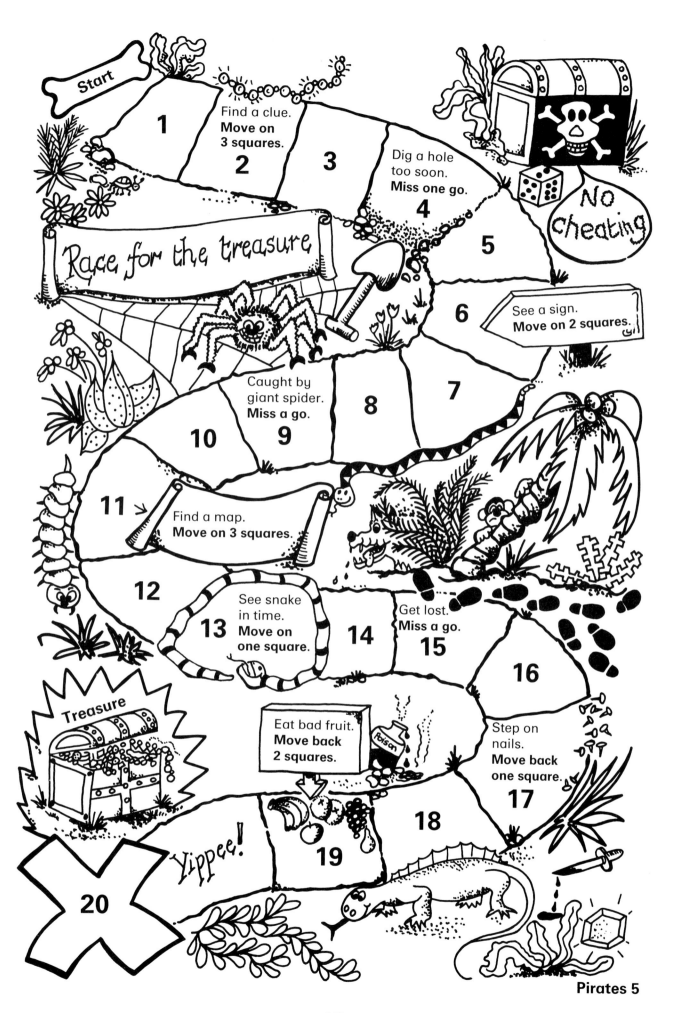

Start

Race for the treasure

1

2 Find a clue. **Move on 3 squares.**

3

4 Dig a hole too soon. **Miss one go.**

5

6 See a sign. **Move on 2 squares.**

No cheating

7

8

9 Caught by giant spider. **Miss a go.**

10

11

Find a map. **Move on 3 squares.**

12

13 See snake in time. **Move on one square.**

14

15 Get lost. **Miss a go.**

16

17 Step on nails. **Move back one square.**

18

19 Eat bad fruit. **Move back 2 squares.**

20

Treasure

Yippee!

Pirates 5

149

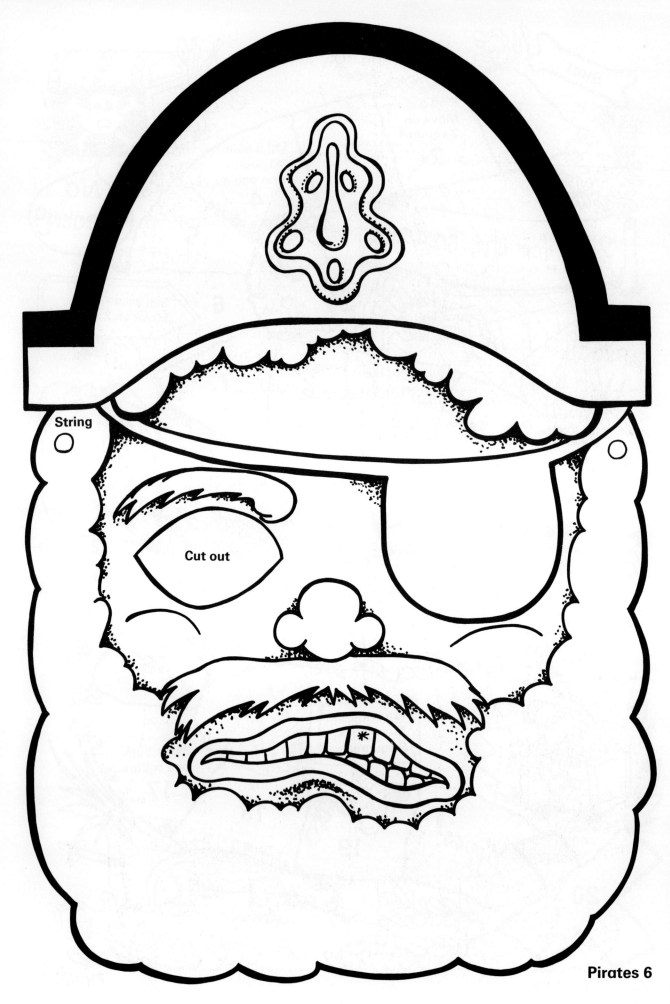

String

Cut out

Pirates 6

150

cut

cut

Pirates 7

151